T0015485

regrets

of

the

dying

regrets

of

the

STORIES AND
WISDOM
THAT REMIND
US HOW
TO LIVE

dying

GEORGINA SCULL

WELBECK

Published in 2022 by Welbeck Non-Fiction Limited,
part of Welbeck Publishing Group.
Based in London and Sydney.
www.welbeckpublishing.com

Typeset by seagulls.net

A CIP catalogue record for this book is available from the British Library

ISBN
Hardback – 978 1 78739 683 8
eBook – 978 1 78739 684 5

Printed and bound in the UK

10 9 8 7 6 5 4 3 2 1

For E, always

Contents

An Opening Note

Some of the regrets you're about to read are very clear and concise. Some are not. Some are quieter, and less assuming. And some, given the circumstances they were borne out of, may not be what you'd expect them to be.

I had two caveats when going out to find people to interview for this book: that they were over the age of 70, or that they were living with a life-limiting illness. My aim was to bring together a collection of first-hand experiences, told from the perspective of those who knew they were facing a finite amount of time left. They came from England, Wales, Northern Ireland, New Zealand and Canada. The youngest was 28, the oldest was 94.

People's health and circumstances will continually change, so I have kept the dates and information correct to the time of each interview.

Some names, ages and locations have been modified for anonymity.

'Tell me, what is it you plan to do
with your one wild and precious life?'

— *Mary Oliver* —

Introduction

IF YOU ONLY HAD ONE YEAR ...

If you only had one year to live, what would you do with it?

If you only had one year to live, would you be happy with the choices you've already made and the life you're already living? Would you be happy with the relationship you're in, with the friends you have, with your health and the body you inhabit, with the work you do?

Is there anything you would change?

Is there anything you think you might regret?

For me, that list of regrets was endless. But I didn't have a year to live, it was much shorter than that. The surgeon who saved me told me the next day that I only had about five minutes left. Five minutes between life and death. It's a hard thing to comprehend, even now.

I was 37 and found myself being wheeled through a never-ending hospital corridor towards an operating room. I'd had an ectopic, a pregnancy where the fertilised egg implants itself in the fallopian tube, rather than your womb, making it rupture and – in my case – causing major internal bleeding.

It was my second ectopic, so I'd lost another baby too. At least now I'd be symmetrical. Tubeless, but in balance.

It's strange, the jumble of things you remember when you can't think straight: the ward sister forcing me to open the curtains every morning, my heart beating a little faster to push my newly acquired blood around my body. Feeling my organs shut down, wanting the pain to end, but also not wanting the doctors to touch me. Realising I was now unable to have more children.

I asked if there was anything else they could do? No, they replied.

I was living in New Zealand at the time with my husband and our two-year-old daughter, having escaped London in search of a better life. And it was better, for a while. On the plane there, I remember looking down at our new country, thinking how I wanted to conquer her. The same way I had wanted to conquer London when I moved back after six long years stuck in a little seaside town on the south coast of England.

It didn't happen, of course, because my life wasn't a mid-budget movie from the 1980s. And I wasn't Michael J. Fox. Or Melanie Griffith.

I was in a relationship that didn't quite work, living in a place where I didn't feel truly comfortable. My work was going nowhere slowly and what little headspace I had left was consumed with trying to have another child.

I felt ordinary. Easily forgettable. Locked into standby mode.

This was not how I imagined things would be.

This was not how I expected to spend my 'one wild and precious life'.

I was born in Central London when the IRA cleared school playgrounds with bomb threats and artists could afford to live there. My dad, who is half-Romani Gypsy, was a sculptor. My mum, a dinner lady. We lived above our nan and grandad's corner shop – a place that not only delivered newspapers to all the big hotels throughout the West End, but also ran an under-the-counter bookies. A step up from my great nan, who was a bare-knuckle fighter around the pubs of Birmingham. (Yes, really.) But I dreamt of something different. Of a fulfilling career. Of a garden full of lupins and hollyhocks, of a house flooded with light. Of being in love. Of motherhood. Of never having to worry about money like my mother had had to worry about money.

Impatient and hungry, I would make rash and risky decisions in a bid to get to my bright and shiny future in the quickest way possible: I ran away from home at 14, got engaged at 15 and moved back to London at 16. On my eighteenth birthday I went to bed and cried. It was as if I could hear time passing, like I could physically feel it slipping through my fingers. I felt I should have done more by now, I should *be* more. Mondays were where diets were born. Bigger plans were reserved for 1 January. Everything good and wonderful seemed to happen in a future I never quite seemed to reach. It was like I was constantly waiting for my real life to start.

This time next year, I would be happy. Maybe.

I'd always kept lists. Lists of things to see, lists of things I wanted to do, all written in bullet point style, ready to be ticked off the second they were completed. They had kept me ordered and on track, but the moment I arrived in that hospital they suddenly felt like a reminder of all the things I'd failed to do. In reality, lots of major boxes had been checked – marriage, home, motherhood – but all I could see were the spaces that remained empty.

After four days and a blood transfusion, I was released from hospital. My body was alive and well, but my mind was struggling. I was lost in a constant fog of questions, reproaching myself for all the things I hadn't done yet and all the years I had 'wasted'.

Was this it? Where had all the time gone, and what had I done with it?

It felt like only yesterday I was sneaking into the Camden Palais or having drunken trolley races down our local high street. Now, I was heading towards 40 with lots of jobs behind me, but no career; lots of addresses lived in, but no place to call home. I knew I should have been happy to be alive. I knew I should have felt grateful, but instead I just felt guilty that I didn't. And every unticked box became a question of 'what if'. What if I had done this? What if I'd made this choice instead of that one? I would watch my daughter do things, hit milestones, and I would think, *I'm so lucky to be here. I'm really, really lucky.* Yet, deep down my overriding thought was, *Why?* Why was I still here if I wasn't going to change things? What was the point of being alive unless I was really going to live?

You'd think I'd become braver. Bigger. More fearless. Well, the honest truth is I didn't. I didn't die at 37, but neither did I really start to live. I'd been given a second chance but I couldn't seem to get going, I just let the fog settle around me.

A year after I was discharged and in the clear, we moved back to the UK. Our daughter started school and my husband set up his own business. Somehow, half a decade had been spent. But I was still stuck in the lonely anger of it all, collecting more and more regrets as the days, weeks and months passed by.

I did try to find a way out.

I joined a netball team; I went to therapy; I made new friends. I tried lots of different ways to try and join in with life again but none of them seemed to work. So, I made a decision: instead of avoiding how I felt, I would face it head-on instead.

I searched for real stories that would remind me that life was something to be cherished. Not necessarily from people who were recovering from a near-death experience like me, or from those who had lived an error-free life, but from people who were perhaps nearing their own end. People who were willing to share, in hindsight, how they felt about the choices they'd made and the things they wanted the rest of us to realise before it's too late.

I travelled the country and telephoned the world, listening to the old, ill and dying talk about life, death and the regrets they had. I wanted to know what mattered as they realised time was running out and what, if anything, they would have done differently.

What you're about to read is an account of those conversations.

Some of these stories are sad and heart-breaking. Some are funny and poignant. But they are all as much about love and life and family as they are about death. More so, in fact. You'll discover their regrets and their mistakes, but mainly their unique perspective on the life they've lived as they face their own mortality.

Ten years ago, I was consumed with regret. The list of things I thought I could have done differently seemed to be never-ending. Now I know how wrong I was, and how unnecessarily hard I was being on myself. What felt like a mistake or a wrong path taken, I can now appreciate as part of a life lived rather than one wasted. And that, after all those compromises and missteps, what we are left with in the end are the things that matter.

The memories we have collected.

The moments we've enjoyed.

And the people that we've loved.

This book is about making sure that the path you're on is the right one for you. I hope that, by the time you turn the last page, that these stories will have helped you as much as they've helped me. I hope every one of them will serve as a reminder to live; that there is usually a reason for the actions and choices we have made.

And I hope that your own tick list becomes a little bit shorter.

Part One

WORK

'Never get so busy making a living
that you forget to make a life.'

— *Dolly Parton* —

Not Doing What You Love

ALAN

I spoke to Alan more than anyone else. We were scheduled to talk on the phone, but the operation he'd had three years ago to try and remove a malignant brain tumour caused some cognitive glitches that can make longer calls tricky.

So, instead, over the next 14 days or so, we emailed back and forth. Me asking lists of questions, him answering, sometimes briefly, sometimes more in depth; typing, as he later told me, while his beloved pug Henry sat loyally at his feet. At times he seemed baffled that I was interested in what he had to say. At others, I think he quite liked getting to talk about the things he didn't usually get to talk about.

The first thing you should know about Alan isn't the fact that he has brain cancer, but that he is probably the most infectiously positive person I've ever met.

He is a marathon runner; he cycles long, long distances; he goes to Oktoberfest in full German lederhosen and he wears his shirts pink. A self-confessed geek, he is an early adopter of technology and a competitive perfectionist. He has been

9

married for 25 years and is the father to two now-adult kids he is very proud of.

But, at the age of 52, knowing that less than 20 per cent[1] of people diagnosed with brain cancer survive more than five years, this isn't quite how he imagined his life would be.

Alan was born into a working-class family in the north-east of England. He grew up in a small rented flat, sharing a bedroom with his younger brother, and was on track to work in a manual, blue-collar job, just like his friends and parents before him. Then, when he was 11, everything changed: his family moved into a council house and his mum managed to get him into a school in a different area, and suddenly, he said, 'I had a lot of friends whose parents were financially better off than mine.'

Seeing the jobs these other parents did, and the money they earnt, challenged his vision of the life he was expected to lead; that he could do something other than work in a factory. He could see the money coming out of London; he could see the yuppie lifestyle he wanted on every advert and TV show. The women would stand in fur coats and high heels, a baby in one arm and a massive mobile phone in the other, the men wore sharp suits and drove fast cars.

It was *The Good Life*, 80s-style, and Alan was hungry for it.

'I wanted deep down to be part of that,' he admitted. 'I must have made up my mind that I wanted a different kind of life.'

Luckily for him, he was a geek born at the right time in history.

'I discovered computers when I was 12 and set about teaching myself how to program. I think in the early 80s anyone who could use a computer was viewed almost as a wizard! I've always had a curious mind,' he added.

At school, he would spend his lunch breaks teaching the teachers how to use their newly acquired computers, but when it came to actually getting a job in tech, they told him it wouldn't be an option. Even his parents wanted him to get a trade, just like everyone else they knew. So, he acquiesced: he left school with a selection of O levels and started an apprenticeship in a local shipyard, training to be a draughtsman.

It was seen as a steady career. And it was, until the government of the day started to privatise all the shipyards and, one by one, they closed. In 1982 the industry employed 62,000 people; within five years that number had dropped to just 5,000.[2] What he'd been sold as a safe and dependable job wasn't, but that downturn gave him a chance to take control and apply for a role as a junior computer programmer at a nearby print company. Finally, his real journey into the world of work had begun and his ambition found a place to grow.

He quickly progressed to the role of analyst, then IT manager.

By the time he hit 30, he had risen to the position of technical director.

A few years later, at the age of 35, he became the youngest CEO in the history of his company and his boyhood dream of a different life had come true. He was earning a very healthy salary, travelling, having big family holidays.

Providing in a way that his parents had never been able to when he was growing up.

'You should have seen my face when I got my first big office that had a sofa *and* a fridge in it. I really did think I'd made it by that point!' he said.

His personal assistant would have a cup of tea ready for him as he arrived at work every morning. His 'big office' would be filled with whiteboards, covered in scribbled notes and ideas. He even had a set of special pens that allowed him to draw and strategise all over the windows.

Alan went from CEO, to COO, to regional MD, to operations director and the head of business transformation, moving on to a bigger part of the business with every step. He was reaping the rewards of that climb, but also feeling the pressure. Pressure to maintain the lifestyle that his family had become used to, and pressure to keep doing what he was doing to secure other people's jobs.

And then as 2017 arrived, what he started was beginning to come to an end. Just not when he imagined it would, and not in the way he had planned.

'I ended up working at our head office on the south coast of England,' he told me. 'A 340-mile-each-way commute that entailed catching the 6.30 train each Monday morning and returning home at 10.30 on a Friday evening.'

His life was spent in hotel rooms, eating the 'wrong food' and drinking too much red wine. He felt burnt out. Exhausted. He hadn't taken a sick day in 20 years; he was used to pushing his body to its limits but somehow this felt different.

'Whether it's the last few miles in a marathon or a 100-mile bike ride, I was used to forcing my body to do things it was protesting about. But even on short training runs of 10k I was having to have a sleep afterwards.'

No matter what he did, he couldn't shake the fatigue, so he did something he'd never done before: he took a break. A sabbatical that would be known as 'the planned mid-life crisis'.

He packed up his office full of scribbled notes. His colleagues gave him cards and presents, they threw him a goodbye party and then he was off. Alan knew it wasn't in his nature to take time away from work, so he donated all of his suits to a local charity shop – to minimise the temptation to look for a new job – and put in place six months of adventures.

'At this point I'd not had more than two weeks off at any one time in 30 years!' he explained. 'It was something I'd always wanted to do, but when I was younger I couldn't afford it and then as the kids got older, there was always pressure at work.

'It just felt like the right time,' he said, then added, 'My family were really supportive.'

He travelled to Cambodia and worked in an elephant sanctuary. He cycled through the South of France, through Girona in Spain. He cycled through some of the climbs used in the Tour de France and other 'epic' places in Europe, snacking on cold beer and cold cuts. He even bought a Porsche – fulfilling a dream he'd had since he was four years old.

But when Alan returned to normality and started a new job, he still didn't feel right.

'I couldn't stay awake,' he recalled. 'I was drinking five cups of coffee just to sustain me at work and as soon as I had dinner at home, I'd be nodding off to sleep.

'I knew there had to be something wrong.'

At first his doctor thought he might have picked up some tropical disease on his recent travels, but when his bloods came back clear, he was sent off to have an MRI scan. And that's when they found the culprit of all his lethargy: a malignant brain tumour, 2cm long; a Grade 2 oligodendroglioma.

'This is going to sound weird,' he said, 'but when they told me, I was more concerned about making the nurse and the consultant feel better. I just thought about how awful it must be to deliver news like this, so I made a joke. Inappropriate for the circumstances, but it helped, I think. I didn't want to be a burden or a victim.'

He then asked the consultant a few questions, jumped back in his company car and headed home to share the news.

'I genuinely didn't think anything was ever going to kill me,' he said. 'I was indestructible. I was the fittest person I knew for my age. I was successful in my career, had no money worries and was what my kids would say, "living my best life".

'I didn't even take out life insurance.'

But looking at the scans in the consultant's office that day, Alan could see something that clearly wasn't supposed to be there.

He thought it would just be a case of opening up his head and scooping out the bad bit, until he was told that the tumour was the 'best type' to get but located in the worst place: nestled between a number of pretty essential areas which, if damaged, would be permanent.

'One area,' he explained, 'was my facial muscles, although that wasn't really a problem as I'm not exactly Brad Pitt. The next was my speech and the concept of language.'

But, he was told, over time many patients manage to recover this element, so again it was less of a worry. For him, the biggest risk was that he could lose all movement in his right side and end up in a wheelchair. He admitted that the prospect of losing physical ability scared him, so he urged the medical staff not to take any risks, even if that meant leaving some of the cancer in there – which is what happened in the end.

I'd heard that some people give their tumours a name. I asked if Alan had.

His answer was an emphatic no. He said he didn't want to give it any more credibility and acknowledgement than it deserved – 'I was determined it wasn't going to change me,' he said.

He didn't give it a name, but whenever he wrote the words 'Tumour' or 'Cancer', he always upgraded them from lower case to upper. Not important enough to name, but not irrelevant enough to ignore, either.

Eleven weeks after his diagnosis, Alan underwent a craniotomy.

Ninety-five per cent of the tumour was removed and he woke up to a train track of metal stitches running across his skull. The first thing he did was try and move his right arm and leg, to make sure they were still working. To his relief, they were.

Overnight, he started to get confused and struggled to talk, but then a new set of meds kicked in and his speech returned. He even managed to walk to the canteen for some cake.

By day five, he was discharged.

After two weeks he returned to his office to attend a board meeting.

And after six he was back full-time and would spend his lunchtimes getting 'zapped' with radiotherapy: radiotherapy that messed with his cognitive ability and short-term memory, leading him to develop epilepsy and lose his driving licence.

Most people at that point would have given up, taken it easy and gone home and rested, but Alan didn't. Instead, a colleague would drive him to work, then in his lunchbreaks he would take a cab to his daily radiotherapy sessions and then three buses to get home. He did this every day for six weeks, followed by six months of chemotherapy.

He admits his expectations were, in hindsight, 'completely unrealistic'.

He had gone from being fit and healthy to having two life-changing illnesses: cancer and epilepsy. From a man used to running marathons to losing muscle mass and gaining 14kg of weight in a short space of time. From the proud owner of a Porsche to someone who had to use public transport. He was left with a 'crater' where the hole was cut into his skull and a patch of hair that didn't grow back after multiple rounds of treatment.

Every aspect of his life had been changed by that 2cm mass.

In the UK, 16,000[3] people each year are diagnosed with brain tumours. In the US that figure is closer to 85,000.[4] The disease kills more children and adults under the age of 40 than any other cancer yet, historically, has only been allocated 1 per cent of the national (UK) spend on cancer research.

It is unknown why one person gets brain cancer and another doesn't. As someone who likes to solve things, Alan struggles with this unknowing.

'Why did I get it when other people who abuse their bodies are fit and healthy?' he questioned. 'Did I cause it somehow?'

He hopes that someday we will know, but right now, all he can do is control what he can control and be honest about his new limitations: that at work he could no longer function at the high level expected of him.

'I had to accept that my career, if I ever had one again, had to change.'

I thought about all of Alan's dreams and ambitions. His compulsion to work and his love of being physically able. The fact that his happy place was running through the woods near his house and hearing his breath and footsteps move through the quiet.

So, how did it feel, losing so much and having to accept this new normal?

'There were certainly some dark moments when I felt I'd been abandoned,' he admitted. 'Like when nobody told me I wouldn't be able to drive for at least 12 months, which actually turned out to be three years. I was expecting to be able to get back behind the wheel after my sick note ran out after six weeks!

'I had no independence. No job, no money coming in.

'We had a very comfortable lifestyle, funded pretty much solely by me, and I went from a really good salary to zero overnight, which I felt incredibly guilty about.

'I never knew if I'd ever get any semblance of my old life back.'

Alan had spent a lot of his working years travelling and being away from home. I wondered, looking back, how he felt about that now.

'I'd be lying if I said it was all miserable. It was certainly lonely, but I had the freedom to do whatever I wanted of an evening. I loved it when I stayed over in London, going out running around the parks and along the Thames. I genuinely miss those days. But,' he confessed, 'it was tough for me mentally.'

At the end of each day, when everyone else went home, he just had a table for one to look forward to. He told me that family was what he missed the most.

'Looking back, I don't think it was worth missing a couple of years of the kids' lives, but on a selfish level, I think the good outweighed the bad.'

I asked Alan if his wife was ambitious, like him.

'She's not ambitious in the slightest,' he said. 'The absolute opposite.'

Like a lot of two-parent families back then, Alan was out working while his wife was at home, looking after their children. Two different worlds that don't always speak the same language. I wondered if his drive and being away so much caused any friction over the years.

'It has caused friction,' he admitted, then added, 'and no, I don't think she understands what I went through to give them a better life.'

He told me about one winter when the snowfall was really bad and the roads were unusable, how he walked 12 miles into work. It took him three and a half hours but he wanted to 'stupidly prove' to those who lived only a mile away that if he could do it, then they could do it too.

Another year he didn't take any holidays off at all, just the national Bank Holidays. 'We were building a new site,' he explained, 'and I foolishly took responsibility for the design and construction, despite already running a business employing 230 people.

'That was quite stressful.'

Now, knowing his time is limited, I asked if he regretted not taking all those holidays.

'I actually do,' he replied, 'but I wanted to be the one that set the example.'

Never taking holidays, not having a sick day in 20 years, wading through heavy snow just to get to work, taking three buses each way while undergoing treatment.

Trying to be the best he can be. Proving himself over and over again.

'I could never switch off,' he said, 'so I was irritable and grumpy at home. I knew that work and family life should be kept separate and I was really proficient at not bringing family issues to work, but was less able not to take work issues home.

'I felt I was defined by my work. Work became my life. The blow-out year of my mid-life crisis was my chance to fit everything in that I wanted to do before starting, what I thought would be, the last phase of my journey to retirement.

'I now have a shorter lifespan than I envisaged and won't be cashing in my pension at 65, so my outlook on life has certainly changed.'

Alan said that his friends and family seem to be in denial about what's going to happen to him. That now he's had the tumour partially removed, they think that his life will just go on, and on. But he knows it's not a matter of if it will grow back, it's a matter of when.

'I think it is their way of coping,' he explained. 'It's probably partly my fault as I don't want to burden them with having to worry about me. I tend to just make a joke about them appreciating me now as I mightn't make it to Christmas! I think they can see my limitations and they understand, although it doesn't stop me thinking I've failed them.'

He feels like he was always the strong one. The one his kids could count on to sort out their problems, and now he doesn't even know if he'll be around to walk his daughter down the aisle, or see his future grandkids. And every few months he has to go for scans to check if the tumour has changed, which understandably can be unsettling.

'At first, I was angry, really angry that I had this. But then I gave my head a wobble. Being angry wasn't going to do anything, I just had to accept that I was going to die sooner than I had hoped.'

People were surprised by his acceptance. They expected him to fight, and battle, and find a way. Maybe because he was the one who always found a solution, the one who fixed things, and this acceptance meant he was admitting that sometimes you can't.

This time, he just had to make the most out of a situation that wasn't of his own making.

Three years on from his operation, he's running again, although not quite as fast. He's cycling too, but not as far. And he's back working, just three days a week as a commercial manager for a much smaller, family-run recruitment company.

Alan is someone who focuses on what he can do, rather than what he can't. But the reality is, everything is harder now.

'My short-term memory is completely shot; my concentration only holds for 45 minutes. I forget to take my medication if I get distracted. I leave lights on, taps on … I need to take notes with me so when I go into a shop, I actually know why I'm there: I must be the biggest purchaser in the country of Post-it notes,' he told me, 'as I have to write everything down!'

He wakes up every day with a headache and has a window of energy – between 10 a.m. and 4 p.m. – before the fatigue sets in.

Once it gets to 7 p.m. his speech can get muddled and he slips into screensaver.

'Having surgery on the brain forces you to question things that you previously wouldn't have given much thought to. Am I the same person I was? Am I thinking the same way

I did? Is my medication affecting the way I think, as well as making me tired?'

Thinking of all the things that have changed made Alan reflect on his work, and what the alternative might have been all those years ago.

'Once you start to earn a lot, it's difficult to do a career change,' he said. 'Once I was on the treadmill, I was worried about how we'd adjust financially, when I just wish I'd stopped and got off.'

I asked what he wished he'd done instead.

'In my own humble opinion,' he replied, 'I think I would have made a great teacher. I would have loved to have worked in a primary school as a general teacher, one who also takes PE lessons. Primary school kids just have a zest for life and learning, which seems to get knocked out of a lot of them by the time they reach secondary school.

'I used to see far too many bad teachers who would write kids off or be really drab and boring. I had so many awful ones and I think kids don't deserve that.'

Getting to know Alan over the last few weeks, I think he's right: he would have been a great teacher. He would have inspired his pupils in all the ways a really good teacher does. But I wondered if there was anything he missed from his old working life.

'You know what?' he said, 'I miss very little, apart from the amazing people.

'I don't miss the stress, the pressure, the being available 24 hours a day, seven days a week. The responsibility for the health, safety and wellbeing of hundreds of people, which used to keep me awake at night.'

There was nothing more he wanted to achieve; he'd managed to do everything he'd set out to do at the start of his working life. He was the youngest director in his group and then the youngest CEO. He had helped build a business that was one of the most efficient and profitable in his industry and the envy of his competitors.

But he knows all of that competitive ambition came at a price.

'It's made me realise that being at the top of an organisation and constantly looking for the next opportunity wasn't as much fun as I thought at the time. It always felt quite lonely when the expectation of everyone in the business was on your shoulders. Now,' he said, 'I realise how much fun I've missed in pursuit of promotion after promotion.

'I think over the years I never once had a "thank you". I was very well rewarded financially, but nobody ever said thanks.'

When he returned to work part-time, Alan swapped his smart suits and matching pocket squares for polo shirts and jeans. His personal assistant was gone, so there were no more cups of tea waiting for him as he arrived in the morning. His office was now an open-plan space.

And this, he tells me, is a good thing.

He says he's happier than ever. That people actually say thank you now and appreciate him; that he has more purpose.

'I get asked a lot about why I continue to work when I have a shortened lifespan. Work is, and always has been, part of my life. To give it up,' he said, 'would mean giving in.

'Bizarrely, I'm a lot more relaxed and happy now, despite having cancer and statistically only having a couple of years to live. I think it's made me a better person. I'm more chilled-out now and tend not to look too far into the future and live in the present.

'It's very much a cliché, but now I really just take things one day at a time.

'I'd love to have travelled more,' he added, 'but that's not really likely now. There are plenty of places I'd like to have visited, mountains to climb and roads to cycle. But when I had the chance, I chose the place I absolutely wanted to visit – Cambodia – so everything else would be second choice anyway.

'I'd probably have Costa Rica on my list, Ethiopia and Australia. But if I don't get there then it won't be something I'd miss or regret. As long as I can get to Paris each July for the years that I'm around to watch the finale of the Tour de France then that will suffice.

'I haven't really got the energy to worry about things that I've not done.

'There's no point looking back at things you can't change,' he told me. 'The only thing you can change is the future. I do wish I'd not been so work focused, sacrificing family time while thinking I was actually giving them a better life, but I've just come to accept things as they are.

'There's always the temptation to say, "Buy that car, go on the holiday – life really is too short, etc." My advice though is not to put all your eggs in one basket. You need to have financial balance. I got it slightly wrong in that I'd planned to do so much when I retired; my financial plan was too back-end loaded. But that did mean when I went to zero earnings, I had a short-term cushion and was able to manage.

'Don't take anything for granted,' he continued. 'Take *all* your leave from work, even if it means just sitting in the garden.

'If you have the chance of a career break, and can afford it, then absolutely take it. Be confident and back yourself that you will get another role when you need to.

'If you want something, and can afford it without going into debt, then buy it.

'The same goes for travel.

'Accept your fate. That doesn't mean stop fighting, but until you accept it then it will absorb all of your energy, energy that you could use to influence what you can change. When I accepted that I won't get to 65, it allowed me to completely recalibrate. What I don't like is when people say, "You might live another 25 years." That would make me a record holder, which would be great, but it's also probably the same odds as winning the lottery.

'The best strategy is to focus on the things that you can control: buy a ticket and if you win, it's a bonus.

'I'm ambivalent to that previous life now,' Alan reflected.

'I wanted the money, I wanted the cars and the nice suits. It took me many years to get to that stage, then just six months of not working to realise I'd wasted most of my life chasing money and not doing something I actually enjoyed!'

Alan would have loved to have been a teacher. He would have loved to have stood in front of a class full of kids and given them something he had to find within himself: the belief that they were enough just the way they were, and that they had absolutely nothing to prove.

His days are now filled with the other things in life he enjoys. Taking Henry out for walks, Saturday night pizza with his wife and kids. Sitting on various charitable boards and supporting other people who find themselves in a similar position to him.

Still looking for mountains to cycle up and forests to run through.

Still challenging himself, but seeing everything old with very new eyes.

'I've been running these trails for the past 10 years and thought I'd known every inch of them. I didn't. All I saw was a few metres in front of me. Processing the data, expunging it out the other end, next data, expunge. One foot then the other, thousands of computations.

'But I've been forced to slow down,' he said. 'To see what's all around me.

'It's a pretty special thing.'

Putting Work First

EDMUND

It all started with a plot of land. A 50-acre section overlooking the ocean where Edmund and his wife would build their dream home and retire in peace. But he hadn't planned on what would happen next; that a stranger would enter their lives and then methodically, and carefully, take away all that he loved and all that he had ever worked for.

Edmund was 87 when we met. He wore a casual suit that wouldn't look out of place at a funeral, a thick patterned jumper breaking up the formality. He'd responded to a notice I put up in an ex-serviceman's club in New Zealand, asking for people who would like to talk to get in touch. A few weeks later a letter arrived. It was brief and simply explained who he was and that he had something to tell me. So, we met up in his small apartment by the coast and he told me about Peter; all the things that happened that he wished he'd been able to stop, and how a decision to work many years before turned out to be the catalyst for it all.

It was the mid-80s in New Zealand when it all started – 1984, 1985. Edmund and his wife, Judy, were getting bored of city life so, in search of a slower pace, they moved to the country, to a place they used to holiday at: rural, remote and 30 kilometres away from the nearest shop. Both were already in their 60s: she was a registered nurse at a medical practice and he had just given up a career in publishing. They were winding down, but Edmund wasn't ready to completely retire, so he joined a real estate company on a commission-only basis, which left him free to come and go.

And that's when that 50-acre section made itself known. The property had been listed with Edmund's estate agents for nearly three years and they hoped, with him being new and ambitious, he would finally be able to sell it.

'It was in four titles,' he said, 'overlooking the beach. The third section of land, the one in the centre, had a 21-year lease, perpetually renewable. All the other ones were much dearer. It had frontage all the way along the Coast Road. Views over the sea, over the estuary. Marvellous views.

'I thought, there I can build a new house and then perhaps my wife would be happier.'

As an added incentive to get him to sell all of the land, the agents offered him a deal: if Edmund managed to get the first three titles sold, then they would offer him the fourth at a reduced price. He said, 'Give me three weeks.' They agreed on a price and the three-week countdown began. Edmund had some 'for sale' signs printed, but by the time he put them up all the sections had been sold. The land was his and now the real work could begin.

A timber company erected, what he described as 'a Queensland-style of home'. Then a separate building was constructed to house two cars, an office for him and a granny annexe for his mother-in-law. Outside, 12 acres of gorse were cleared from the land, fenced off and subdivided into 13 paddocks. An orchard was created and a garden was planted full of freesias and daffodils. For Edmund, it was a beautiful pay-off for a lifetime of hard work.

'I used to look out every night, out at the view, and think how lucky I was. And then,' he said, 'I met Peter.'

Being a bit older, Edmund decided not to work the property himself, so he placed an ad in the local paper, offering some of the land for grazing. He got two replies: one from a farmer he didn't know, and the other one was from Peter.

Peter had built a small house on his farm two plots away, so he was already a near neighbour. In the beginning, Edmund liked him. Respected him, almost.

'I thought he was well presented,' Edmund said. 'A reasonable conversationalist. An efficient farmer by the look of things and had plenty of equipment. I really thought he was quite a good bloke.'

So, they signed an agreement that allowed Peter to graze the land for a year, stocking it with young beef, which he raised to a certain age and then sold off; cutting a thousand bales of hay off the property. Making an income.

After that first year they just carried on 'in trust'. Then Peter met Edmund's newly divorced daughter, started calling in on her and helping out around her property, and a few years later he got divorced and moved in: Peter and Edmund's daughter were now a couple, and a very close one.

Edmund said everything was okay until there was an opportunity to freehold his land. He told me that he intended to keep his house and the view that he loved so much, but sell a large portion of the rest. Knowing it had become a desirable plot, and hunting for a quick sale, Edmund went to all of his nearest farmers first and asked if they'd be interested. But while he was out, visiting a possible buyer, he received a phone call from his wife. She told Edmund not to do anything, because Peter was with her and he 'had a plan'.

So, Edmund went back to the house and Peter put forward this plan. A plan that would allow Peter to buy all of the freehold and whatever profits were left after the sales would be divided between them, 50:50. He could do it because he had all the equipment that Edmund didn't have to prepare the ground before putting it on the market.

But the plan didn't quite go as expected: Peter managed to sell the first two sections, but Edmund never got to see any of the money. He got nothing but bills, bills that were somehow paid out of his and his wife's joint bank account.

'Peter charged me for the council permit,' he said. 'He charged me for his surveyors, his lawyers, the gate gadget, freight on metal … He charged me interest on all the expenditure, including the money he borrowed from the bank to pay for the freehold. He even charged the grazing on my own land against the subdivision. I pulled out of the deal before the third section came up. I didn't trust him after that. I suppose he got so used to the land it became a part of him. I was suspicious, but Judy, my wife, kept saying, "He's a nice boy."

'But how,' Edmund wondered, 'could he cash a cheque to pay for all these things unless it was endorsed by us? I gather my wife signed the documents for him.'

Edmund and Judy had been married for over 40 years by that point. They met in London, in 1954. He'd decided to go over for the Queen's Coronation, but before he went, he had to have his appendix out. And that's where they met: she was a nurse in the hospital. He left the ward never expecting to see her again and sailed for England.

'Well,' he said, 'a sea voyage is great. You get on an airliner and your brother could be on it and you would have no idea. But on a sea voyage, you get to know people.'

And the person he got to know was the nurse he never thought he'd see again: because they happened to be on the same boat.

'So, there we are,' he noted. 'It was co-incidental. And with a lot of the coincidences in life, the unexpected always happens.'

They went to the Coronation together, and then both stayed on in the UK to work.

I asked Edmund, 'What was she like?'

'She seemed like a sensible person,' he said. 'And funny enough, I thought, *she can type too.*' Then he smiled and added: 'And that's handy, because I'm not very fast.'

They kept in touch and were married eight months later.

So, was it love?

He said, 'Well, it was an affinity. A compatibility at first sight.'

But there was one element of their union that wasn't quite so compatible: Edmund was Rh positive and she was Rh negative. A clash of blood types that led to two of their children being stillborn and to the difficult delivery of their only child, their daughter. By the time she was two years old, and with only £19 in his pocket, they decided to move away from the wind and rain of England, back home to New Zealand.

I kept thinking how hard that must have been. Going home and starting again, this time with a wife and child to provide for.

I asked how he would describe himself?

He paused for a moment, thinking, and then replied, 'As, probably determined.'

His childhood was typical for, what the American journalist Tom Brokaw would call, The Greatest Generation. The men and women who grew up in the Great Depression and lived through 'The Good War' of World War II. It wasn't easy, none of it was.

'My father died the year I was born, so I've had to stand on my own two feet. Life was pretty hard, quite frankly. It was a pretty hard upbringing.' He said he could remember he and his brother living in a Salvation Army home for unwanted children. Of a row of boys, one by one being put into a bath, scrubbed clean and then passed on to the next person, ready to dry them off. 'I can remember that vividly,' he laughed, before adding, 'I was about four or five, I guess. I don't know where my mother was.'

There wasn't much money about in those days, so as a child, Edmund used to strip the copper sheathings off boats for cash and search the streets for bottles and cans to collect for refunds. But he wasn't the only one struggling: lots of people were in the same position. The doorways of empty buildings were awash with the homeless and Edmund said he would look at them and say to himself: 'That will never happen to me. You had to make it or you'd just be another one of the poor.'

As I tried to imagine what life must have been like for Edmund, his brother, and countless other children all those years ago, he steered us back to the reason I was there: to the moment when Peter had sold off those two sections of land and Edmund had changed his mind about the third.

'I got so fed up, I said I wouldn't sign any agreement with regard to any further calculations with Peter Gibbs. I didn't trust him. And what I couldn't understand is, every time I said something against him, my wife just kept saying, "He's a nice boy." Then she came up with a proposition to pay for the university education for the grandchildren.'

Edmund said they held a meeting at his house and his daughter explained that she couldn't pay for their university fees, but selling that third section of his land could. She asked if he would do it for her; she asked him to trust her.

'And I looked her in the eye,' he said, 'and thought, *You've only got one, you can't have any more and you've lost two*. I thought, *Well, if you can't trust your own daughter, what's the point?*

'Then my wife said, "If you don't sign this agreement, you won't be able to subdivide anything 'cause I will not sign the papers." So, I said, "All right." But it didn't get paid to my daughter. I said to my daughter, "What happened?"

'She said, "Peter's got all the money."'

Peter had received all the funds and was drip-feeding it to her; he had taken control.

Then the couple decided to get married and hold the ceremony at the family home. It was a small affair of about 20 people, mainly members of Peter's family. Edmund wasn't invited, but attended anyway. He said he felt like an onlooker: 'Peter commandeered my daughter's place,' he said, 'and now he was commandeering mine. What could I do? Just keep an eye on it, that's all.'

The relationship between Edmund and Peter became more and more strained, with his wife and daughter standing in Peter's corner at every opportunity. And then, one day, it all came to a head when Peter asked him another question about money that would end it all: 'He said, "Why can't you let your daughter have her inheritance now?" It had really become antagonistic,' he admitted. 'I had a lounge, 18-foot long, and they would stand at one end and I would sit in the other, being got at by people who I once trusted and didn't trust anymore.

'I once said to my wife I wouldn't stay in a bitter marriage, so I felt that was her trying to make the marriage so bitter that I would walk out and leave the farm and everything. I really had to hang on until I could find some way of getting out of it with half the value of the property.'

Edmund's wife didn't speak to him for six weeks after that last conversation and when he bumped into his daughter out and about in their township, he'd say hello, but she would pretend he was invisible and walk off.

In the end, he sold his house. To his daughter. And to Peter.

'I told her, if she could come up with the money, which I knew was really if Peter could come up with the money, I'll not stay here.'

So, a price was agreed upon and the sale was signed. Just like the sale was signed on the other plots he'd lost control of.

Edmund went away for the weekend, to take a break from it all, and by the time he got back all his pot plants were gone, his dog was gone and his wife had temporarily disappeared, in an effort to avoid being involved in the move. He was informed by his wife's lawyer that the payment for his half of the property would be made available in one week, but there was one stipulation: they would require occupation within those seven days. Seven days to sort out and move a lifetime's worth of equipment and personal effects, and to vacate the property.

And that was that: he moved out of the home he had built and into a one-room bedsit.

'I decided that under the circumstances I must divorce my wife and disown my daughter because of their behaviour,' he said. 'Because I thought by disowning her, I was disowning him too.'

He had become a husband without a wife, a father without a child and a landowner without any land. By the time his divorce was final, he had been married for 48 years.

Edmund admitted that, over the years, he's found himself pondering why his daughter betrayed him and his wife lied.

'If those two children had lived, we would have been a normal family,' he said. 'My daughter would have had company. But she sought company from a large family, which I haven't got. What she did had huge repercussions. "Trust me, Dad," she said. "Trust me." I would have carried on out of loyalty but there wasn't much point if there wasn't any loyalty on the other side.

'I asked her one day, I said to my wife, "Why did you do this to me?" She said, "Because you provided a home for my mother. And now my mother's dead, I don't need you anymore." Her mother lived with us for 30 years and I never charged her a bean.

'I think my wife was weakened. A lot of factors came into it, thinking it through now.'

One of the main factors occurred a couple of decades before, after his wife had lost their two children and had gone into hospital for a hysterectomy. Edmund was working for a publisher at the time and had a lot of meetings already scheduled. Worried about losing the potential business, he didn't feel able to cancel them, so his wife went to hospital on her own. He said he offered to show her the agreements to back up his argument that he had to go, that it was hard to find the 'right man' to talk to.

'I had to call at the right time of year when they got their allocation of advertising budgets. It had to be perfect timing. I knew if I didn't appear at that time I'd be lost. So, I said, "Look, Judy, I'm sorry about this but I have to go because I've scheduled appointments which I must keep or it's the end of my business." It got cool after that. And then as my daughter grew up, she got a bit cool towards me, too.

'I thought, *Well, you don't just throw away your intended livelihood.* I didn't have the education that Judy got, but I did equip myself over the years in my own way. Life was pretty hard, quite frankly. Getting vouchers for food, collecting bottles. You had to make it or you'd just be another one of the poor.

'So I went. I had to. And I feel that's been held against me.'

He believed that decision, to not be there when she needed him the most, was still felt decades afterwards. He was understandably worried about losing his livelihood, losing all that he'd built, but ended up losing it all anyway.

Every year, about a week or so before the rest of the family gathers for Christmas, his grandchildren take him out for a meal somewhere. But, he said, they keep him at arm's length.

'My granddaughter says, "I've got to be loyal to my mother." And my grandson says, "I don't like what happened, but I don't want to get involved." They are not aware of it all. I don't think even my daughter knows the way I struggled to get a publishing career. She was only young then. I knew what I had to do, to make a success of it. And, if I had let my emotions rule my life, then I wouldn't have had a business.'

Edmund's life is very different now. He has moved into a new house and community. He likes to keep himself occupied, so he goes to Scottish dancing on a Tuesday and square dancing every Thursday. He says that he will dance with the ladies but not get involved.

He has rebuilt his life as best he could, but still finds himself looking back.

He told me about the day he called in on the place he once called home and found that their land had been sold off to a timber company and four additional houses had been built.

He said 'they' had a long-term plan and that long-term plan had paid off.

'But, what can I do about it now?' he asked.

All these years later, he was still mulling it over. Still contemplating how he could take Peter, his ex-wife and his estranged daughter to court, to get back the dream he had lost through trusting people he realised he could no longer trust anymore.

'I'm angry,' he said. 'It churns me up. I've been working on putting things together. I write it down, all the dates and everything like that. I should be able to whip it into shape, because after all, I whipped into shape the career journal, the textile journal and the retailer's journal. From nothing, from not being a publisher.

'But then again, I'm twice as old now. I am 87. If I was 40 years younger … And so you're a victim of time. Time marches on without you. But shall we say, from a pretty tough childhood, I made it and I lost it.

'I've lost my whole family, I've lost my property. I've lost everything. Very few people know what happened. They think, perhaps, I've been widowed but I have not stated. Well, it stirs me up inside. Who do I talk to?

'Everyone thought he was a very nice chap.

'Everyone still does, I think.'

Working Too Much

ADA

Ada lived up the road from my paternal grandparents. In a neighbourhood full of show homes and gravel driveways, she was the most like them: someone who had also escaped their dusty beginnings. She came from a generation of women who worked for need rather than ambition, but she was a mixture of both of those things, because her need was the thing that drove her: there was never enough food in the cupboards, she only had one pair of shoes she had to share with her younger sister, and she had to get a job and leave school at 14 so she could help her family out financially.

But Ada wanted something different: she wanted more.

And slowly, gradually, she got it. She married a steady, constant man and, together, after a number of failures, set up a business that worked. It wasn't her grand passion – she didn't love it, just like she didn't really love him, but it meant they could have a 'good' life.

The couple bought a big house with a swimming pool and accumulated a driveway full of cars. They joined the golf club and the bowls club and distanced themselves from the clambering world they had both come from. Children arrived, three of them, but neither Ada nor her husband had the bandwidth to be parents; their main focus was creating a fiscal safety net big enough and strong enough so they would never have to worry about money ever again.

So, they worked. Twelve hours a day, seven days a week. They moved 16, 17, 18 times; pivoting from house to house and business to business, trying to create something successful. There were no evenings together, or holidays away; there was no time.

She was retired and in her 70s when we finally got to meet during a chance encounter outside of my nan's house. I'd been told so much about her over the years, I found myself saying how amazing it was that she had managed to create so much out of so little.

Her response was as unexpected as it was short: 'I'm not sure if any of it was worth it,' she said. Ada died of pneumonia before we could sit down and really talk.

I never saw her again.

Not Having a Good Work-Life Balance

NIALL

The year 2020 was the year the world stayed at home. It was the year the streets emptied and the hospitals filled. And it was the year Niall Murphy nearly didn't make it.

A 43-year-old human rights lawyer from Northern Ireland, Niall had travelled to New York City for work in early March. But when he returned to Belfast a week later, he brought home more than a cheeky bag of duty-free. He brought home a case of Covid-19, a virus that would change so much for so many of us. It nearly made his wife a widow, it nearly made his three children fatherless. And it gave him a second chance at life.

He is a tall, thick-set man with closely cropped hair who commands the space around him. His voice is a melodic dance of 'you knows' that at times feels more suited to a musical score.

We got to speak about five months into his recovery, after he'd had time to process what had happened to him and was due to return to work. He started by explaining how he felt when he got home from that trip overseas, recalling the times and dates with exact legal-like precision: how he flew

REGRETS OF THE DYING

back on the Wednesday evening, went to his daughter's First Confession on the Thursday and was back in his office for a big case on Friday.

And it was that Friday when the virus really hit him hard.

'The first symptom arrived with me at 8 p.m.,' he recalled. 'I'd never, ever felt an illness like it, just a terrifying exhaustion. I was totally bedridden.'

Niall had developed a very high temperature. He had no appetite, no energy. By day 10, a stream of uncontrollable coughing had arrived. And that was when he was admitted into hospital.

'I could almost feel my hamstrings tightening, just lusting for oxygen,' he said. 'I actually felt I was going to die because I was coughing so much I couldn't get my breath back in. I remember stamping on the floor, just trying to stimulate some sort of breath. It felt as if you were being drowned.'

Covid distancing rules meant that Niall had to enter the hospital alone while his wife sat in the car park outside, hanging on, as the doctors checked his blood pressure, temperature and oxygen levels and made the decision to intubate him.

'If I'm being honest,' he admits, 'I didn't quite know what ventilation was. I thought it was like a glorified oxygen mask, I just didn't know that it was so invasive, right down into your lungs. I didn't know that I was going to be hooked up to a feeding tube and a water tube and a medicine tube.

'I also didn't know the death rate.'

Niall managed to call his wife to let her know what was happening before he was taken to the operating room and then, as if he was simply having a tooth removed, he counted backwards from 10 and drifted into an induced coma.

For the next couple of weeks his wife and children waited at home for news, not knowing how long he would be under, hooked up to a bank of machines, his body punctured with tubes that were doing what he was unable to do alone: function. He had a 50:50 chance of surviving, odds that started to tip against him when his bowels began to fail: 'There was a chance that I was going to die,' he said. 'I was in a coma and obviously was completely oblivious to everything, you know. My wife had to endure that.'

Then, 16 days later, he woke up.

He had no idea he'd been 'out' for so long, he said it felt more like hours. But the state of his body told another story: he had lost 30lb in weight, 25 per cent of his muscle mass and had an 85 per cent deterioration in tendon functionality, which in turn led to general exhaustion and weakness.

He found himself sitting on a gurney, halfway along a hospital corridor surrounded by nursing staff head-to-toe in full personal protective equipment (PPE) clapping his arrival back into the real world.

'I genuinely thought in my own head, *I'll just get my clothes on and my wife will collect me and that'll be me on my way home*. I said to the nurse wheeling me, I said, "Okay, so have you got my clothes?" And she sort of looked at me and said, "Why, what for?" I had no understanding about a recovery period.' In an effort to try and make Niall fully grasp his current situation, the nurse got him up and let him take a few steps on his own. He only managed three or four before he gave up; his legs could no longer carry him. He admitted, 'Those few steps felt like a marathon.'

It took another month of rehab before he was finally able to go home to his family.

Niall was the first on his ward of 26 patients to survive Covid-19. In fact, he was the first person in Northern Ireland to make it off a ventilator alive.

Many of us die without knowing how our friends and family really feel. We may have had an inkling, but sometimes we're not given the benefit of time to truly express how much the deceased meant to us, in all the big ways and all the small; in the way that they were, or in the things that they did. The grief pours out and alongside it all the love and anecdotes that might have been shared while they were still alive. But for Niall, this wasn't the case. Because one of his work colleagues put a call out for people to send emails and texts, sharing how they felt about him as he lay intubated and unaware.

Messages flooded in, over 3,000 of them. He likened it to a wake for the living.

'An Irish wake is a mythical, majestical thing,' he said, 'where the deceased is celebrated and talked about, and it felt like dropping into my own wake, having all these expressions of goodwill and positivity. Being able to hear all the things people would say. I actually got to drop in and read all that, and that was very uplifting and positive.'

He said it was like being emotionally catapulted forward. That it enabled him to 'surf the goodwill' and help him rationalise why he made it out alive.

'I have been told by consultants that, you know, they were getting prepared for another statistic. So that's quite … knowing that that was you … Most people don't know when they're going to go, but to have walked into the hospital with all your wits about you and then to be put under a voluntary coma, not knowing – I might never have known that I had died because the plug would have been pulled out and that would have been it.

'That's a bit difficult to wrap your head round,' he admits.

When you've been on a ward of emptying beds and you're the first one to make it out alive, you could also be left with a lot of 'why did I survive and they didn't?' type questions, questions that may never be answered. Niall was warned this might happen, but he says, so far, he's been able to rationalise it: 'I'm computing it almost as a flash illness,' he said, 'and I've got out the other side of it and it's gone and it's never coming back. I'm going to be okay. I've family and friends who do have serious illnesses like motor neurone disease or cancer, and it's just horrendous. So, as bad as it was, I just try to rationalise it all as a glass half-full.'

Niall became infected with the coronavirus in the first few months of the pandemic, when doctors and scientists were still scrambling to understand what it was and how to treat it. As I'm writing this, over four million[5] homes will now have an empty place at their table, so he knows he's one of the lucky ones. But how does it feel to get another chance? To know that you've been given the time to rebuild your life, if you want to?

Second chances bring into focus the ticking clock that most of us try to ignore. They can force us to accept that the life we have will not go on forever. They can help clarify what is really important to us – and also what isn't. And because of that, second chances can affect people in many different ways.

Niall is, by any measure, a successful man: he is a partner in a law firm, he has a family, a happy marriage; he set up a new Irish language school that now has 213 pupils; he has helped raise over £2 million to build a new local sports centre. I wondered whether he'd have any regrets at all, given the amount he had already achieved in his life, and if his near-death experience made him realise the need to change things.

It did, and it has. Because for Niall, being so close to death was 'like hitting reset'.

'My life was exceptionally busy and chaotic,' he admitted. 'And going forward, it's not going to be as busy and chaotic. The time that I was able to spend in recovery, ironically it was almost some of the best time of my life, because I was able to spend so much of it in the house with my kids. I had never had the opportunity to do that before. And that was a sharp intake of breath, you know, having a daughter who is seven and she's a comedienne and I didn't appreciate how much craic she was or how funny she was. I got it in small snippets, but she's just a welcome hilarity and I only got that when I was locked down for 24 hours a day.'

Like most of us, Niall usually works full-time. He leaves home first thing in the morning and his family life has to exist in that thin pocket between dinner-time and bed. And now that thin pocket doesn't seem enough somehow.

'You realise how much you miss at home. At best, you're getting home at six, the kids go to bed at nine, so you're only really getting two or three hours a night with them. When you realise how different a lifestyle can be, it is a bit of a reset in terms of what's life all about and what you want to get out of it.'

He says he's learnt to 'cherish every moment and minute you have, not ever take anything for granted, and to love and hold and squeeze the ones that are closest to you'.

And then his mind switched back to work and a case that was waiting for his attention: a 14-year-old boy, Noah Donohoe, whose body had been found down a storm drain. Noah's mother sought out Niall's help to look into what happened, to engage in the investigation and to represent her at the inquest. The teenager went to the same school as his eldest son, so he felt compelled to help.

'It really sharpens into focus, you know, just how precious life and relationships are. So, in terms of lessons learnt – it really sharpens into focus, you know, just how precious life and relationships are. Not that I ever took anything for granted, but I would go that extra mile, value and appreciate all the positive, good features that I'm blessed to have. And that's not a feature of everyone's life and I appreciate that. But it just sharpens into focus how lucky I am and have been.

'There's a personal responsibility in that as well,' he added. 'We all have the opportunity to do and achieve great things. You determine the path, the forks in the road at every juncture.'

And that's where I left him. A man who had survived. A father who had been given a second chance. Covid-19 had slowed the whole world, nearly killed him, then forced him to slow down, too. But now he was on the other side of it, did he want to reinvent his life? Did he want to start again?

The honest answer was no, not really. He was already living a pretty good life, a life he liked. Part of me was expecting him to lament the amount of time he'd spent at work and on community projects that must have taken him away from his family. But he didn't regret any of that. Maybe because his job has a wider purpose: it wasn't just about creating money and climbing some ambitious ladder, it was about helping other people.

But what his near-death experience did do was shake him up. It allowed him to refocus and open up to the possibilities of what could be, to create a better balance between work and home, and to appreciate what he already had just that little bit more.

'I'm looking forward to the second half of what I've got to offer the world,' he said. 'I know how lucky I am and that's just going to inform everything going forward, you know?

'Life really is the most precious gift. It's over in a flash. And it should not, cannot, be taken for granted.'

Part Two

FAMILY AND FRIENDS

'Every human being, of whatever origin,
of whatever station, deserves respect.
We must each respect others
even as we respect ourselves.'

— *Ralph Waldo Emerson* —

Last Words Said

CHARLI

Sometimes the regrets we feel most keenly are bound to us by grief. They are the things said or unsaid, done or undone, to someone who is no longer here to receive our apologies. It's the type of regret that can be the hardest to process because there is no easy way back. There is no phone you can pick up to talk. There are no hugs to be had, or tears to be shared, because they are gone.

This is what happened to Charli.

She went to sleep on a good day and woke up to a nightmare.

It was the summer of '93. She was 21 and at university. A pretty, petite blonde with everything in front of her. Her parents had divorced the year before, so her family was fractured: Charli away from home for the first time, her younger sister still living with her mum and her younger brother, James, working for their dad's flooring business in another city.

Charli explained how, after years of living in a marriage that didn't quite work, her parents' divorce enabled her dad to build a life that brought him some happiness. He had a social life again, and girlfriends. He even bought himself a motorbike.

I asked if maybe he was having a mid-life crisis?

'No,' she said. 'I think my dad was experiencing freedom. I think he'd been very unhappy with my mum. She'd had affairs for years and this final one – with our family solicitor – was the nail in the coffin. Dad had a motorbike when we were little but my mum didn't want him to have one, so of course when the divorce happened …'

When the divorce happened, he could do – and buy – whatever he wanted.

On the night of the accident, her dad and brother had been riding to the coast to join Charli's nan for dinner, then James planned to go out with friends. But none of that would happen, because her dad made a decision that would change the course of their lives forever.

'My dad let my brother drive,' she explained. 'My dad let my brother drive, and …'

Charli struggled to find the right words, repositioning her sentence, none of them seeming to fit: 'And he was – it wasn't – he hadn't – he wasn't legally allowed to drive it. He was only 18 and he hadn't passed his proper motorbike test, so it was illegal. And it was 1100cc, incredibly powerful.'

The pair were seen riding out of their village, her dad sitting at the back, riding pillion. All was okay until they were a few miles from their destination and James went to overtake a car and lost control.

He'd been in a number of crashes before, but this time, with a bike this powerful, James ran out of luck: he crashed head-on into another car, fell into the road and was run over by a passing vehicle. His dad was thrown from the back seat into a ditch, away from the oncoming danger, but the force of his fall was so great he sustained a serious head injury that would affect his speech, make him unable to function and confine him to a wheelchair for the rest of his life.

James was taken to hospital, but he died two hours later.

He died before anyone could get there to say goodbye. He died alone.

The police tracked down Charli's mum and informed her what had happened. She told Charli's sister, who then told Charli. Her phone rang at quarter to midnight and she said: 'At that point what I heard was "James is dead and Dad's in intensive care." I didn't know anything else.'

Her family still had to identify the body.

Charli said she had what can only be described as an 'animal response', grabbed all the photos she could find of her brother and drove to him. She felt that she had to take care of it. To be the strong one so that no one else had to.

'His eyes were still open,' she said. 'And what I see in that now is that he wasn't there. He'd gone, his spirit had gone. His body was there, his eyes … his eyes were open, but his life, everything that makes a human a human, was gone. It was horrendous.'

'That was the night of 2 July 1993,' she said, then added, 'The rest is difficult.'

With her parents divorced, and Charli being her dad's oldest living child, all the decisions surrounding his care fell to her: 'Because I was the next of kin, they were asking me to make decisions about taking my dad's leg off, amputating his leg, turning the life support machine off. All this stuff.'

She laughed nervously, noting, 'I didn't smoke or drink before then.'

Sometimes we tell lies to help insulate people from the truth, to try and make things easier so they can cope with the hard stuff. And that's the difficult thing Charli was referring to. Because when the police took her to identify her brother's body, they admitted that her dad hadn't been the one driving.

'They said to me, "We know that your brother was driving the bike. We don't feel we can sue your dad or take him to court because he's very ill, so the papers are going to say that your dad was driving."'

The trouble was, only Charli and her dad knew the truth.

'That was really, really hard because I knew that my dad was lying. I knew that the police knew, or that they'd told him to lie because they didn't want to prosecute him. But I knew that my mother, whose son had just died, didn't.'

A couple of months after James was laid to rest, Charli and her mum went to see a medium. Charli remembers sitting in a room and the medium telling them that James had made contact and that he had revealed that it was him who was driving. Charli laughed again, recalling how her mum cut in, insisting he wasn't, while she just sat there, 'screaming, in my head, to my brother in heaven, "Don't tell her!"'

Charli lived with that secret for over a year. Then her dad, wracked with guilt, tried to kill himself. And when he became stronger, she took him aside and told him that she couldn't keep his secret anymore, that it wasn't fair on her; that it was just too much. In the end, her dad told the truth: 'He just couldn't live with it,' she admitted. 'He couldn't live with what had happened and what he felt he'd done.'

So, Charli's dad told her mum and the secret was out.

I asked Charli what James was like. She described a tall, skinny guy who had lots of friends and fell in love easily. Someone who was into clubbing, listening to Lenny Kravitz and reading poetry. She said he was very, very funny and very sensitive, but that there was also lots she couldn't remember.

'I don't know what he used to love or hate. Or what food or drink he liked, or what posters he had up in his bedroom. My memories of him have faded. I can't remember the little things, those things growing up. I can kind of remember when I look at a photo of him, but the older the photo gets, the more blurred they get.

'What I have is the love that doesn't change,' she added. 'A memory can fade, but that love isn't moveable. That love is something I feel very, very strongly. So, my memory is of a spirit rather than a physical being.

'In terms of regret …' Charli paused briefly, centring herself. And then she told me.

I thought it might have been going to identify her brother, or keeping the secret of who was driving the bike for her dad. But it was neither of those things: it was something she said, the last time she saw James alive.

Two weeks before he died, he'd been to visit her. And after a 'great' night out, she'd dropped him back at the local train station so he could get home and pick up his car at the other end. But halfway through the journey, he realised he'd left his keys at her house so he jumped on the next train back, calling Charli from a phone box to come and meet him.

'I went back to get him, and we went back to my house to get his car keys, and then back to the station. And in a jokey way I said, "And don't come back again."

'Which of course, he didn't.

'So, that is like one of those things that you say in jest, joking, hugging, not realising. Because if he'd lived, I'd have forgotten that I ever said that. It would have been neutral to me. It wouldn't have even been on my radar. But because he died and that was still fresh in my mind, it stayed in my head and always has.'

Over the years, her acceptance of what happened has changed, but she admits that she would often go into rages with her father, mainly because she was the one left to care for him.

'I had been a daddy's girl,' she said, 'and I really struggled with looking after him, taking care of him, doing what I should be doing because there was no one else. And feeling incredible resentment and anger towards him for being responsible, in my mind at that young age, for changing my life so irreparably, forever. And it did, and it has.

'It was like I couldn't really grieve for my brother because I went straight into looking after my father, and I was doing that for 20 hours a day in that first eight, nine months.'

Charli didn't just help him physically. With his vocal cords damaged in the crash, her dad had also lost the ability to speak, so she would lipread and speak for him, relaying his needs and wants to whatever medical staff were there.

The pressure lifted slightly when he started to get some home care, and then near the end, when he moved into a nursing home. But if anything needed to be done, or needed to be decided upon, Charli was it. She admits it left her with 'an incredible anger' towards her dad and she still finds herself wondering why he let her brother take control of his bike that day. Her dad was stocky and strong, but James was different, he was tall and skinny. He wasn't very experienced at driving, let alone riding a bike. But he looked up to his dad; he wanted to be like him. So, where he led, James followed.

'He'd already had five crashes in his car,' she recalled. 'But my dad just kept buying him another one, buying him another one, buying him another one. He was young, he was inexperienced. He was driving too fast.'

I asked if that day was the first time he had let her brother ride the bike?

'I actually don't know the answer to that,' she replied. 'I don't know. I suspect it wasn't, but who knows?'

Over the next two decades or so, Charli went through various stages of trying to cope. She started smoking, started drinking; took drugs. She was forced to drop out of her course at university to care for her dad and gradually lost herself in all of the above. She was married for a few years; had Zak, her now-adult son whom she adores. And when she managed to get back to education, she trained as an addiction nurse, then as a personal trainer, where she managed to create a community of women who would come together, in all weathers, and exercise outside.

She buried her heart in whatever she was doing, using it to take her away from how she really felt. And at the same time, her dad was 'deeply depressed' as he battled his own guilt. His suicide attempt a year after the accident was the first in a long line of many and with every new attempt he would make, and every time a motorbike roared passed her in the street, Charli would slide back into that night. Of hearing about the crash, of viewing her brother's body. Back to the start of the secret and the pressure on her to be the one left to cope.

She found herself living between two parallels: between being Charlotte and Charli.

'I was able to mentally create this separation. "Charlotte" looked after her dad, whereas "Charli" was the woman I always thought I wanted to be.' She confessed it was part of a mask she wore, not realising she could be both women at the same time.

Her dad was 48 when the accident happened – the same age Charli is now.

They were 'linked completely emotionally' until the day he died.

She had been his carer longer than she had been solely his daughter. And now she was free, just like her dad had found himself free after his divorce. Knowing he'd been ill for so long and was needing more and more care, and that he was the last living piece of that accident all those years before, I wondered how she felt when he finally died.

Was she, in a way, relieved?

'I'd been sort of praying for him to die,' she admitted. 'I'd had enough, I'd had enough of seeing him in pain. I would never have told anyone this at the time, but yes, I was wishing he would die, but not wishing he would die so there was a paradox. You know, like loads of people say, "I hope it was peaceful". Well, it was anything but peaceful, right up until that last breath. And all the while I'm praying for him, talking to him, "Please let go, let go, let go. I can't do this anymore." It didn't mean I didn't love him,' she added. 'It didn't mean that I wanted him to die, but I just couldn't bear to see him in pain anymore. I'd just had enough.

'I wanted it over, I wanted to be released.

"I loved him very much but I didn't know who I was anymore. I didn't know where to go, what to do, who to take care of. That moment when I drove back on the night of 1993, where I went into that "I'm going to sort this out" mindset … I did that for 20-odd years. I'd drunk my way through it, smoked my way through it, exercised my way through it, starved my way through it, workaholicked my way through it, and when my dad died, I just completely gave everything up. I just collapsed into it and surrendered into it, because I'd run from it for 20-odd years and I couldn't run anymore.'

It's now been 27 years since Charli lost James, and three since her dad died.

Some friends have stayed by her side, supporting her. Others have fallen away.

Every year she posts a picture of her brother on her Facebook page. She finds that no one talks about him anymore, so it's her way of marking the occasion and of reminding people that there was once a blonde, handsome teenager who had his life cut short. Someone she loved and loves. People understand and remember then. They comment and click 'like' and 'care'. And then all falls silent until the next year.

They say that grief is what happens when love has no place to go. For Charli, grief also brought its own share of regrets. After her dad died, she wanted to break free from all the things that had kept her confined to that life of duty and care. So, she sold her house and sold her business, and went travelling, trying to work out what should come next. But by the time the dust settled, she found herself without the community she'd created, and without the house she had called home.

And then, she realised that she'd made a terrible mistake.

'Living in the regret of selling my house was suffocating,' she said. 'I was flying high on the wings of – I'm not working, I'm having a break, I'm travelling, I'm going to India. I'm doing this, that and the other. And then it started to sink in, what I'd done: I'd given my money away and we didn't have a home anymore.

'I lived in that regret and it was awful, absolutely horrendous. And if I think about it now, I can still feel it. I can feel the grief and pain in that decision.'

She still felt the weight of those decisions made so soon after her dad's death, but she also accepted that, like the crash, there was no way back from it.

'On reflection, the living in regret is awful. Nothing good comes from that place, does it? Because it's gone, it's in the past and we are all doing the best we can do in that moment. I wish I'd known what I know now when my dad was alive because I wouldn't have been so harsh on him or resentful for the decision that he made that changed my life.

'I don't know. Maybe it was all meant to happen like it did for me to get to this point of self-acceptance.'

I asked if there was a difference between the regret Charli felt about her last words to her brother and the regret her dad felt, letting him ride his bike. She went quiet for a moment, then replied: 'I don't regret his decision,' she said. 'I feel angry but I can't regret it because they weren't my decisions to make.

'My regret was I said this last thing to my brother, but like I said, if he had lived, I would have forgotten that I ever said that. It would have been neutral to me.'

She had jokingly told him 'and don't come back again' and in a way, saying those five little words, at that particular moment, meant he would never ever leave.

She ran through all the things that had happened and how one thing had led to another, half wondering if any of the steps had been different, would the outcome have been different, too? If her mum hadn't had the affair, then she and her dad wouldn't have split up, and then her dad wouldn't have bought the motorbike. And if her dad hadn't bought the motorbike …

'If, if, if,' she said. 'If, if, if.

'I do regret not having a lifetime with my brother. I do regret not being able to say goodbye to him. I do regret not being able to get to the hospital quick enough to be with him when he died. But again, those sorts of things are out of my control.

'It was all out of my control.'

During the course of these interviews I have found myself thinking more and more about this idea of control. About the things we have the power to change and the things we do not. How we can find ourselves inheriting the pieces of what's left, even though we didn't have the control to stop the break in the first place; and how we then carry them with us, clutching them tightly, trying not to drop the tiniest of fragments. Charli did that for years, for decades. She carried the pieces through love, and divorce; through building up a business, and selling it on; through having a child and then watching him grow up and forge his own life.

But in the end, she had to set the pieces down.

'I don't believe I'm broken anymore. I don't define myself by that grief anymore. That very visceral, debilitating grief and regret no longer … I can see it for what it is. It doesn't mean anything about me. And that's the misunderstanding, isn't it? That when we have a regret, like my dad, it's like "I've done something wrong". I did this. There's something wrong with me and I'm broken because I'm disabled and my son is dead.

'And here's all the evidence that I am not good enough.

'I'm not frightened of that pain anymore,' she added. 'I'm not living in a place of *you're to blame, you're to blame, if only, if only* … I lived there for too long, my dad was there his whole life. And you know, my dad didn't mean for my brother to do that. No one would have made that decision, it was just an accident.'

With the help of therapy, good friends and the passing of time, Charli has gradually, finally, found a way to live with her grief and with all the regrets that surround it.

She became free and then she freed herself.

'I think you can get drawn into "I'm a victim" when actually it is just what's happened. It's either one big mess or one divine intervention to get me, for whatever reason, on this path. I can feel pissed off and angry and sad. If I dig deep, it makes me upset, but I don't want to be upset anymore.

'I've felt upset since I was 21. I'm 48 now, it's a long time. My whole life, you know? But I'm now better than I've ever been,' she said.

'It is, I guess, what's made me who I am.'

Missing Out on the Future

TASSIA

The future is a place we take for granted. We imagine what it will look like, and what it will contain, but in reality, it's a place not all of us will reach. Tassia is one of those people. She's in her 20s and is living with a disease that will end her life 50 years sooner than she'd planned.

We connected through her blog 'Pink Is Not My Colour', an online journal she set up to talk about her situation. On the opening page sits a picture of her, shaking a cocktail, happy and smiling; a banner statement typed across the centre: 'It is not about dying with cancer ... but how you choose to live with it'.

We started with all the things she loves: horse riding, mountain biking, big rooms filled with loud music, people, parties. Her two cats and one dog. Her partner, Nick.

And art. Tassia loves art.

Most of us can probably remember the moment when we made a connection that stuck. For Tassia, it was when she decided to wander into Tate Britain – the grand porticoed gallery in

London that houses many of the UK's most recognisable pieces of art. She recalled how she walked into a curved room and in front of her was a triptych of huge orange paintings.

'I was alone,' she said, 'and I became acutely aware of my own heartbeat. I recognised the twisted, contorted, grotesque figures of a Francis Bacon piece, "The Crucifixion". I had only ever seen it in a book but here it was, in front of me.'

She grew up on a council estate in South Wales, in the shadow of a steelworks. There was a beautiful coast and beautiful mountains, but there were no galleries, or easy access to them. Her love of art started when she discovered the work of the conceptual artist Gillian Wearing and the way she uses film, performance and photography. Tassia confessed: 'It wasn't like anything I had ever seen before. I had a fairly turbulent childhood, and for me, art became more than just doodling dragons. It became a way to let out potentially dangerous thought processes.'

She said it gave her another way of expressing herself when she couldn't articulate her thoughts and feelings in words alone. But until she walked into that curved room engulfed in orange, books were the only real gateway she had to the world of art. She already knew she loved the work of Bacon and Wearing distantly, on paper. Now she realised just how much. So, she moved to Bristol to study art, but before she left, she discovered her next love: Nick.

They met in a nightclub when she was just 18. He came and sat next to her and asked for her number. The next day, they started texting. And from that point on they were together, sometimes physically apart, but always a team: both studying and working; touring the UK on their bikes, cycling through northern France and Belgium and back.

'We had nothing but a paper map, a few clothes and a tent. It was so freeing,' she said. 'So much fun.'

She also travelled to the US twice, went on an exchange placement to Hong Kong and travelled around Northern Taiwan, all on her own.

'I got the idea of doing a Master of Arts abroad from this. I loved the adventure.'

Once she and Nick had finished their degrees at Bristol, they planned to save up a bit more money and move overseas; to travel through Europe, then settle in Copenhagen or Amsterdam. Tassia would study towards her MA and continue to make cocktails in the evening to make money, while her partner, Nick, would teach. Then, in October 2015, she felt a hard lump in her left armpit. Over the next couple of months her breast would feel achy, but she dismissed it, thinking it was nothing. Then, when she went to her GP for something else unrelated, she mentioned it and the doctor took a closer look and found two more lumps.

'The same day I got referred for my breast lump was the same day we went to view a campervan. We were going to sell our furniture, and just go. Start in France, travel south, over the Alps, Italy, Switzerland, Germany and end up in Scandinavia. A few good months of travelling and getting a "feel" for places. We just wanted to explore, people-watch, cycle, hike.

'After my biopsy and ultrasound, I had "a feeling",' she said. 'It sounds like a cliché but I think I may have picked up on the doctor's concern. I was sent away to wait for my results for a week, but I knew ... I felt it deep down.'

After some more tests, she was diagnosed with breast cancer. She was 24.

'When I was told I had cancer I was quite calm, I had already begun to process it.'

Tassia had multiple treatments, but the cancer came back. She recalls the moment she knew something was seriously wrong: she was having physio for a bad back and it wasn't working, so she was referred to have a kidney scan but collapsed before it could happen.

'I was driving Nick to work and had to stop to be sick. The retching was so violent, I fell from the car and blacked out a little. When I came to, I was paralysed. The pain was just ... no words.'

Nick got her to the emergency room and after 14 hours she had the official confirmation: the cancer had spread, and it was now terminal.

She expected Nick to leave her but instead he took care of her and they became even more of a partnership. 'We are opposites,' she told me. 'He is steady, consistent and calm, I am fairly up and down, but we have always been a bit of a team.'

A year before her diagnosis, he surprised her with a trip to the English coast. And in a room overlooking the sea, just as she was unpacking her bags, he popped the question.

'I turned around and he was on one knee. I said, "No, I don't know." I was 23 and needed time to think. But by the end of the trip, I felt I wanted to be with him forever.'

'Nick is the love of my life,' she added. 'He is my absolute rock.'

The pair agreed to have a long engagement and not to rush into things. They had no idea that 12 months later, Tassia would find a lump on her breast that would be cancerous and that four years after that, the cancer would spread and metastasise around her body, making her cancer inoperable.

Now, 11 years after exchanging numbers in that crowded nightclub, they've decided to have a small 'legal' wedding in case she 'goes downhill and doesn't recover' and then have a big party in the summer. Not a standard wedding with hats and vol au vents, but a real celebration.

'I want to make sure everyone is comfortable and has a good time,' she told me. 'We have very little money but a lot of friends so instead of presents they're going to help. I know a chef, a photographer, a DJ, several cocktail bartenders and a friend of a friend owns a big farm, where we plan to have it. I even have someone to do our cake!'

She said she feels very lucky.

After her diagnosis, they moved back home. Back to the shadows of the steelworks, overlooking Swansea Bay. Back to the quiet part of town. The horses are still there, but she's now unable to ride them because her bones are too brittle after multiple rounds of chemo.

Your 20s are an age usually reserved for having fun, trying to work out who you are and what you want to do with your life, not thinking about your life ending. Not having to adjust to all the things that are different to the way you imagined they would be.

'You do think about your life a lot when you know you're dying,' Tassia says. 'Physically, I have changed a bit,' she admits. She's still 5ft 4 with ginger hair, but now, post-chemo, it's been cut, from a bob into a very short pixie. She still loves wearing colourful clothes; she's still very outgoing, energetic and curious.

'Cancer can become your identity after a while,' she said. 'You lose the version of you, you have carefully constructed over the years. I still feel like me, but many elements of my identity were taken away with each diagnosis. It is amazing how much is tied up in your job and your ability to do certain things.

'If I never got cancer, I like to think I would have achieved a PhD. I wanted to become a fine art lecturer and tutor,' she added.

She told me that she wanted other people to experience how she felt when she discovered Gillian Wearing. She wanted the hairs on the backs of their necks to stand up just like hers had, seeing those three paintings by Francis Bacon hanging side by side. She wanted them to become trance-like, listening to a language without words. A language she believed anyone and everyone can understand. That's why Tassia wanted to become a tutor: to encourage people from all backgrounds to see the value in art and to help 'sweep away' the pretentiousness that can be so off-putting to so many of us.

'But my life took a different turn,' she explained. 'After cancer, I had to make every decision to keep me near the NHS, so I stayed, and art took a back seat. I am stuck.'

She stayed in the UK. And she stayed in her job in cocktails and was promoted to development manager; which meant travelling the length of the UK, teaching other bartenders how to make the 400 drinks she knows how to make; the drinks she would have been making in Copenhagen or Amsterdam if she hadn't found that lump and had been able to hire that campervan instead.

'I don't regret anything that was in my power,' she said.

What she regretted were the things that she couldn't do now she was ill. That she couldn't study abroad, that she couldn't travel; that she couldn't ride her bike or the horse that she loved. But, looking back, she was happy that she'd done so much before she'd developed cancer. She was happy that she'd toured through Europe on her bike when she could. She was happy she'd gone to Hong Kong, and Taiwan, and the US. That she might have found herself 'stuck' back in Wales, back in her old life, working in the world of cocktails and bars, but she loved both of those things, so they made her happy too.

I asked if she knew what her prognosis was, right now.

She told me: 'The average lifespan for someone diagnosed with Stage 4, metastatic breast cancer in the UK is just two to three years. I am one year in. I hope I will live longer. I have lost eight friends from my cancer community in the last five months and seven of them did not know it was coming: one minute we were talking and the next I got the news. My last friend to die went into hospital and never came home – not knowing she wouldn't come home. That really scares me. I feel like I could be dead next week and not know.

'I am gutted I am not even 30 and am planning my funeral. I feel robbed.'

I asked what she wanted healthy people to know and what things she will miss.

'People really need to stop taking themselves so seriously and think about how their actions impact the world. I wish people would just be happy and grateful for what they have because they may not know they're living their last best moment until it has passed.

'When I die, I will miss taking deep breaths of fresh air, watching the sunset and feeling the wind on my cheeks. I'll miss cuddles with my cats and the company of my partner. I will miss a cancer-free life. A chance to live life the way I wanted.

'I will miss being alive,' she added.

Tassia is the kind of person who likes to sit at a bar and buy the waiting staff drinks. She is the kind of person who stays up with friends, having deep conversations until the early hours. She is the first one on the dance floor and the last one off. Life will miss her, too.

Some of the people I've spoken to have told me they felt more able to say no to things after getting a terminal diagnosis, and to back away from people who didn't make them happy. I wondered if this was true for Tassia.

'Nope,' she replied. 'I've always adopted a "live for the now" mantra, so I've never done a job I didn't enjoy and never had relationships I didn't like. I just wish that I had known that 2015 would be my last "cancer-free" year.

'I would have really made the most of everything!'

Not Looking After Your Health

TOM

Litter was strewn throughout the hallway, ankle-deep. It was like a bin had been tipped over and the contents just left there to be trampled down. I had spent five hours on a train to get to him, but my first 10 minutes with Tom were spent stood outside of his front door, with him apologising profusely for the mess and me reassuring him that I really didn't care.

I was there because two years ago Tom was given two years to live and he wanted to talk. Weighing in at nearly 500lb, he is what the doctors would call 'super morbidly obese'. He struggles to walk, struggles to breathe, and after breaking multiple beds, spends his days and nights in a sunken lazyboy, facing a massive 60in TV screen.

But somehow, he's still with us. As a religious man, Tom considers this a 'miracle'.

He is a kind, thoughtful 29-year-old, who still lives at home with his mum and little brother. His weight has always been a problem. A problem that has caused other problems. At school, he was bullied. And now, as an adult, on the rare occasion when he does manage to venture down the single flight of steps from his flat to the outside world, he is heckled by strangers. When he recounts these moments of uncaring, he never fully repeats what people have shouted, the swears and curses are edited out. Our conversation kept strictly PG-13.

'I've been battling with my weight since I was six years old,' he told me. 'I've been on different diets, done loads of exercise, but I still put weight on.'

I asked if anyone else in his family was big, like him.

'No, there's only me,' he said.

He was keen to illustrate what he eats and reeled off a list of 'healthy' foods and highlighted which ones he has for breakfast, lunch and dinner. He also talked about the consumption of things that are completely off the menu, but not for medical reasons.

'I don't drink alcohol,' he explained. 'I go to the Church of Jesus Christ of Latter-day Saints – Mormons – and you're not allowed to drink alcohol, tea, coffee, not allowed to smoke. The only drugs I can have are from the GP or the hospital. There are very strict rules. Can't have sex before marriage, you have to get married before that.

'If you go on dates, a member of the Church goes with you.'

'Have you ever been on a date before?' I asked.

'That's one of my low points,' he replied. The answer was no. He'd never been on a date, or even kissed a girl.

Tom isn't completely housebound yet, but the flight of stairs between his flat and the street below has become increas-

NOT LOOKING AFTER YOUR HEALTH

ingly hard to conquer. He used to play rugby, he used to swim, he used to go to church. He used to do lots of things but gradually his world has become resigned to that broken chair in his bedroom and playing PlayStation 1, then 2, then 3, then 4.

Eating salads and jacket potatoes. Trying to 'be good'. Everything changing but him.

'Sometimes I worry about the future,' he said, 'and sometimes you can't think too far ahead. You have to keep to the present day. Like, each day comes when it comes. I plan everything the day before, not like months or years before.

'I feel ashamed about my life,' he confessed. 'It does seem a waste being like this, although I'm trying to lose weight. It's my own fault; 50 per cent I don't deserve it, 50 per cent I do. I think it's my mistake and I've got to live with it.

'I've been taught at church, it's like a test. For me to do the right thing or wrong thing.'

I asked him to clarify what he meant by 'right' or 'wrong'. He explained that he meant having better control over the food he ate. Like the control he had already exercised by not drinking, not smoking, or drinking tea or coffee. And then, as if in confession, his already soft voice fell a little softer and he admitted that sometimes, once a month or so, he would binge on big bottles of cola and bags of potato crisps (the remnants of which could be felt scattered underfoot).

At the age he's at, one year shy of 30, Tom is different to all the other younger people I'd met. Because he says he's not scared of dying, or even really worried about it. His religious beliefs as a Mormon, seated in the idea of reincarnation, seem to have taken away any justifiable fear he might have had. Because when he dies, he believes that God will give him another go around. That a second life is waiting.

'I think to myself, if I do die, I can go to heaven, then come back reincarnated and put stuff right. Stay active, eat the right foods and go to the gym. I'd be much better, I'd be much thinner. I'd have a wife and kids as well.

'If I do die,' he added, 'I'll get to see my relatives who have passed before me.'

Near the end of our chat, I heard a key in the front door. It was Tom's mum. A short, straight-sized woman carrying home a few bags of shopping. She joined us for a moment and I introduced myself. There was no mention of the rubbish that covered Tom's bedroom floor, nor the clearing I'd had to make before sitting down. She just said hello and then left us to it.

This was her normal. Which made it Tom's normal, too.

Seeing his mum bringing home those bags of food prompted me to ask: 'Who cooks?'

'She cooks,' he said, 'but I overshadow her. I'm worried she might do it the quick way, in the deep fat fryer.'

Tom relies on his mum and others to help him cook meals because he has learning difficulties. 'I can't read properly,' he told me. 'I can't write properly. I can't do stuff on my own. A few things I can understand, about playing on computers, and trains. Everything else I can't.'

There are many things that Tom is unable to do, but if he lives long enough, the things he wants to try and the things he wants to fill his life with are as simple as they are universal.

'I'd like to travel,' he told me. 'I'd like to lose a bit of weight, get myself a passport and go to America or to Australia. I'd like to go to New Zealand. I'd like to meet a nice lady who accepts me for what I am, what size I am, and helps me to lose weight.

'Be understanding and help me prepare my meals.

'I'd like to go on walks, and hold hands and stuff.'

Putting Yourself Last

DEE

Help yourself first, they say. Help yourself first or you won't be in a position to help anyone else. This is the instruction you're given on a plane when the safety video starts to play. The air stewards point out the emergency exits, they show you where the life jackets are and they remind you to put on your own oxygen mask first. It's logical advice. Logical, and clear.

But in our day-to-day lives, few of us do this.

Our natural instinct is to help and to be there for others in a way we rarely are for ourselves. If our partner needs us, we're ready. If our friends need to talk, we listen. If our children need anything, we will do whatever it takes to make sure those needs are met. This is the stuff of life: helping others, being part of something bigger. While this is an inherently good thing, it can also mean that we place ourselves so far down our priority list that we put everyone else's needs above our own. In our actions, in our choices, and in our lives.

Just like Dee had.

I met Dee through a Facebook group I'm part of, one of those places you dip in and out of every once in a while. The collection of members is mainly older and our talk often drifts into issues of health and happiness, so I shared that I was looking for people to interview and she got in touch.

At first, she wanted to talk about being estranged from her son. But by the time we spoke, she'd realised her regrets were much wider than that; that they encompassed many different elements of her 75 years of life. That there had been a series of events, one after another, where Dee had put her own oxygen mask on last. Something she regretted now.

Born in 1945, she was an only child, raised by her grandparents who ran a little bakery in rural Kent. Listening to her describe her life back then, on a superficial level at least, it sounded idyllic: she went to a small school with only three classes, her village had a little sweet shop in it, a pub, and a post office; neighbours would share any extra fruit and veg they grew.

They lived in a large detached house which stood on the village square; the bakery on the ground floor and their five-bedroom home on the floor above. Dee used to sleep in the smallest room at the back.

I asked her to describe her grandparents to me. What they looked like and how they were.

'My grandma always wore dresses with those pinafores that go over your head and are tied round the waist. And stockings,' she said, 'rolled over just above the knee.' Her grandfather had a best pair of trousers and a best jacket. Once a week he'd go out to the local Working Men's Club for a drink and wear his best flat cap. Their days were long and hot, and started at 3.30 in the morning when the coal-fired ovens in the kitchen had to be lit.

There were some idyllic aspects to Dee's life, but being at home wasn't one of them.

'The atmosphere when I was a child was very cold and very critical,' she told me. 'My grandmother, in particular, was a very cold woman. She didn't like little girls. She told me if I hadn't been born, there wouldn't have been all the problems in the family.'

Dee didn't mention her parents, so I asked where they were.

'I don't know,' she replied. 'I don't know what happened to them. I was born at the end of the war and there were lots of children who didn't have parents for all sorts of reasons.'

Her parents just disappeared one day and left her to her grandparents. Grandparents who seemed very reluctant to be forced back into the position of parenthood.

Dee told me that one day her grandmother handed her a little booklet, full of pictures of sunshine and happy kids.

'I can remember her saying, "Would you like to go to this lovely country, Australia?"'

Her grandmother was trying to sell her the idea of moving to the other side of the world. Those bright, coloured images must have seemed like paradise compared to 1950s Britain, but Dee didn't see it that way, because she knew they wouldn't be immigrating as a family; she would be expected to make the one-way trip on her own, freeing her grandparents of any responsibility they had been lumbered with.

In the end, she stayed in the UK. But the coldness and constant nit-picking continued, and set Dee off on a pattern of trying to make everyone else happy but herself.

She admits that there must have been a reason why her grandmother was the way she was, but she never did find out. Because at 17, Dee had had enough and moved to London. She managed to find somewhere to live and secured a job as a filing clerk; life stayed like that for a while, making friends and making rent. And then she met the man who would become her husband and father to her only child. She was 23 at the time.

'We met at a gig at Imperial College,' she told me. 'His band was the support. He was a drummer and had a lot of confidence, and that appealed to me.

'He had dark hair and blue eyes,' she added.

Dee directed me to a video clip on YouTube of one of his old bands. An all-male group, with all the usual instruments and standard short but scruffy haircuts. Her ex is stood at the back, playing a set of bongo drums; he was exactly how she described him.

She explained that he was poor but ambitious and had grand plans for a career in music. So, by the time their baby was born, instead of staying at home with her son like Dee wanted, or working on the things in life that she wanted to work on, she supported his dreams instead and went back out to work.

'Someone had to bring in the money,' she said, 'and it was me.

'He was very ruthless. Maybe if I'd had more streaks of ruthlessness I might have survived better, I don't know. But he wanted something different, so he went and found it.'

And while Dee was out at work all day, her son was passed on to another family member to care for him: her husband's mother, her son's grandmother.

Dee admitted, 'She absolutely adored him, and he adored her.'

The pair were connected by Dee's absence. An absence created by the need for money, and by Dee putting herself last.

The marriage lasted for three years until her husband hit her a couple of times and she decided to leave. But Dee encouraged her ex and his family to stay in her son's life, for his sake, and their childcare arrangement continued.

So, everything was repeated. Her grandmother raised her, and now her son's grandmother was helping to raise him. Her mother-in-law squeezed into the space between her and her son. And as other things were added to that squeeze, an estrangement gradually took hold.

The final cracks developed when Dee decided to move away from London.

Her son was already a young adult; she was 52, had been made redundant and was struggling to find another job. She was about to lose her house and needed to find a cheaper way of living so it seemed like a good plan, but her son did not approve. He couldn't understand why she was unable to find employment in the city, or why she had to move so far away. Basically, he just couldn't understand.

'You know how young people can be,' she said. 'Just go and get another job! And I said, well, you know, it's not that easy.' He didn't seem to realise that she was competing with other people half her age, who would work for a fraction of her salary.

And then her son met someone online, an American woman who, Dee said was 'very clever, very bright, but also very possessive, and very opinionated.'

The couple got married, and the mother and son drifted even further apart.

'I can remember my son saying that his wife felt that family shouldn't be involved with their marriage and that neither should I. That they were a unit. And I have to say, they do live in a sort of bubble. I mean, they do seem happy.

'My son loves his job,' she added. 'And she likes her job, but she doesn't like me.'

The closeness Dee and her son had felt in the early days, the closeness that had already become frayed when his grandmother stepped in to help with his care, became even more so. He started making excuses about why he couldn't see her; he would complain that the journey was too far, that it was too difficult. And gradually, he stopped travelling down to see her.

Instinctively, Dee knew that if she pushed for a real reason, then there would be an 'almighty row' and her son would take his wife's side.

'That's how it would be,' she noted, 'because if he didn't, there'd be all hell to pay.

'The problem is, they've been married now for 12 years: is your son really going to turn round one day and admit that he's been a prat for the last 12 years? Because he's not, of course he's not. And the easiest thing has been for him to side with her for the peace and quiet, and gradually to distance himself from me. Which is what he's done.

'I mean … how does this fit in with my regrets?'

I gently reminded her that she originally got in touch because she wanted to talk about her son, and her thoughts drifted back to those early days, back to before other people entered their maternal bubble. Back to before the cracks started to embed.

'I was determined when I was pregnant that I was going to do my very best to be the best mother I could be, and to give my son the things I hadn't had; birthday parties and all sorts of things. I didn't envisage having to go out to work. But I look back now,' she told me, 'and think, well, yes, it's pretty obvious really that if my son was spending a lot of his formative years with his grandmother, he would get very attached to her.

'I thought it would be fine,' she added.

I wondered if her son was like her ex-husband.

'In lots of ways, yes,' she said. 'But that's fine. I think I would rather he was like he was, and be able to survive in this world, than be like me who's struggled.'

Dee has come to the conclusion not everyone out there will treat you the way you treat them and she's glad her son knows that, because she wished she'd known it sooner. Or rather, she wished she had acted on what she had already known, deep down.

'I think we all have this instinct thing where we know if someone is lying to us. But when I'd say, I honestly feel there's something wrong here, people would say, "Well, where's your evidence? Where's your evidence that it's wrong? Where's your evidence that's happening?" And then I'd think, I haven't got any.'

It takes confidence to believe in what you feel. Now Dee knows to listen to her gut and to go with what feels right. But she can't undo all the other times she didn't, especially in the early days when she was so much younger and hadn't yet built the confidence to discover who she could be and what she was really capable of. She said it was 'difficult now, at my age, to look back and try and unscramble that childhood mind'.

'My grandmother adored this little girl who lived up the road and she used to say to me, "Why can't you be more like Elizabeth? She's such a lovely little girl, such a good girl." And I'd look at this Elizabeth and what I saw was this dainty little child with big blue eyes and blonde hair, whereas I was quite clumsy with red hair and freckles and brown eyes.'

Dee thought that maybe if her hair colour was different, that if *she* was different in some way, then her grandmother would think she was a nice person; someone worthy of her time and love. And that by default she wasn't enough just the way she was.

When Dee went to university as a mature student, she studied psychology. There, among many other things, she learnt about the concept of the 'good penny, bad penny' and how some children can be seen as bad pennies and some are seen as good, even though there's no real basis for it. But once that label is stuck and repeated enough times, it's hard not to believe that it's not true on some level. Just like when we tell ourselves we're stupid, or silly, we say it so often, we no longer realise we're saying it and then we believe it as gospel.

'Of course, when I was old enough to understand it, I could see that I would never have been able to do anything right, no matter how hard I tried. And I did try. It was just because, you know, she wished I wasn't there.

'But as a child you internalise it,' she noted. 'You don't really know what it's all about but you internalise it. So, there was a lot of coldness and a huge amount of criticism.'

Now Dee is older, she admits that she can see certain aspects of her grandparents' life in a way that she couldn't when she was young. She told me that her grandmother helped out in their bakery, alongside having to do all of the housework and childcare while her grandfather spent long, hard hours in a hot kitchen on his feet.

'It was a very busy life,' she said. 'And I know my grandfather had very bad legs, so he was always in a considerable amount of pain. I used to see that in his face.'

Getting older isn't something we talk about much in the Western world. We tend to pretend it isn't happening until we can pretend no longer. I remember my grandmother saying she still felt like she was 27, until she looked in the mirror and got a bit of a reality shock. I know I find myself doing the same thing now. But when your health declines, you may not need a mirror to tell you things have changed: it's something your body communicates very loud and clear, and unmistakably.

'There's not much difference between being in your late 60s and being 75,' Dee told me. 'I mean, when I turned 75, I thought, I don't feel any different from when I was 74, or even when I was 70. But at 65 I looked quite young and I was quite fit and the pain wasn't that bad. I was actually enjoying life very much.

'But it suddenly … People think pain just gets worse and worse and worse and worse. It does, but pain also takes jumps. You know, you're going along nicely and it's almost like one day you wake up and – oh! You are in a bit more pain and you become a little bit more disabled, and walking at a certain pace is not possible any longer; walking for a length of time isn't possible any longer, without severe discomfort. And that's what I've noticed: these little increases or these little hops and jumps you hardly notice, and then one day you do.

'I'm a relatively young old woman,' she added, 'but my brain …'

Dee paused, realising she'd used the wrong word, and restarted with the right one.

'My *pain*,' she said, 'still affects me, it still affects how my memory works. I mean, I struggle now with words.'

And words are the things that Dee holds most dear. You start as a child not talking, using gestures and noises to express what you want and how you feel. And then you say your first words, then learn more, and more, and then they sit there, ready to be pulled out and used in conversation: in anger, in happiness, and in joy.

Dee always had a large and expansive Rolodex of vocabulary at her disposal, yet now she struggles to find the right words and admits that really upsets her, mainly because there's nothing she can do about it, but also because it's another area of possibility that she felt her circumstances blocked her from fully exploring: writing.

She told me about the time she won a writing competition when she was 14 and at secondary school. All the children were asked to write an essay about 'why they bought a poppy for Remembrance Day' and when the headmistress called Dee into her office a few days later, she assumed the worst.

'I went in and thought, oh my God, what have I done? And then she told me that I'd won. I just looked so stunned. And she said, "You didn't expect to win, did you?"'

Dee was very proud of that win. Nearly 60 years later, she still is. Unfortunately, once again, her grandmother didn't feel the same. She refused to come to the prize-giving ceremony, she just told Dee it was a waste of time.

And then, after she left home, other people's needs and wants got in the way and Dee 'wasted' less and less of her time writing. She used to try and get some pages done in the evenings, after work, but found it hard; living in a succession of bedsits and flat-shares that were too busy and too noisy for her to concentrate in. Then she had her son and found herself juggling his needs with those of her husband.

Her dreams, once again, set aside to allow her (now) ex-husband to be free to chase his.

She felt trapped by her circumstances. The last one on the list, always.

'If I'd had the luxury of having a bit of money behind me,' she said, 'I would have just concentrated on writing. But the need to survive got in the way of that and it became such a habit that when the chance to dedicate myself to it came, I just didn't take it. I wish I had. I wish I could have arranged my life differently … I suppose that's one thing I feel that could have been different.'

I asked how she imagined her life would be now, if she'd gone down that road and really made a go of it. Would she be happier? More content?

'Oh, I think I'd be a lot happier. I mean, I'm not unhappy,' she clarified, 'I'm not terribly unhappy. But, I just wish I could have done it. I wish … Well, we all need to have compassion, but you can't let it get out of control, which I did. And I wish I could have had more confidence in myself, because then I would have put everything more in balance.

'But there were a lot of areas in my life that were out of balance.

'Certainly, from my generation, that's how women were encouraged to be. Very much the givers and the homebuilders and the carers, and taught to put yourself last. Someone once said, "God first, others next, self last" and that's what women were encouraged to do in my day. You couldn't be too clever. You couldn't be too smart. You couldn't be too funny.

'It was good that you had a sense of humour but if you started being witty or a bit funny, people did not like it, especially then. Now it is different. Men appreciate humour. I still think women are often expected to be more caring, more understanding, but perhaps not to the degree that they're giving everything of themselves.'

Dee has had a few relationships over the years, but none of them have stuck. She admits that she finds it hard to trust people; another thing, in hindsight, that she now connects with her childhood. She said she never settled down because 'there's always been that element of, well, this person might go away'. Like her parents did; like her grandparents tried to do with their attempts to send her to Australia when she was young.

She now realises what she may have missed out on.

There was one man in particular that came to mind. She was in her late 30s, divorced and a single parent; he was much older and had three ex-wives, all of whom he was still friends with. He even proposed marriage, but she declined.

What was he like? I asked.

'He wasn't my usual cup of tea,' she told me. 'He was an Old Etonian. He was just charming, and he just loved me for what I was.

'He actually pointed out to me once, he said, "Why are you denying that you're worth loving?" And I remember getting really upset and saying, "I'm not denying it." And he said, "But you are. You're an absolutely fantastic person and yet you're behaving as though you don't deserve to be loved."

'I still regret that I didn't take him up on his offer. He bought me a ring and everything and I didn't take him up on it and I regret it to hell now. He was a fantastic bloke.'

They were getting on really well, but she couldn't shake the thought: what if it all goes wrong? What happens if he leaves me? 'I'd always thought all these negative things,' she admitted, 'so I just started pulling back.'

There was another factor that can't have helped, either: he liked her son, but her son wasn't very keen on him.

For a while, they kept in contact. But then she met someone she described as 'totally unsuitable' and married them instead. The Old Etonian wished her well and hoped she would be happy. Three years later, he died of cancer.

'I knew when I heard he was dead, I thought, You fool, you let that one go.

'Christ, why did you throw him away? But that's how it is. It's recognising love, and if you don't, you don't. I mean, if you're loved then you feel confident. If someone loves you … I said to someone once, if I feel loved, I can do anything. And it's true. If I feel I'm genuinely loved, I could fly to the moon. But if you're not loved …

'If I'd had a normal family life, if I'd had a mother and father and been brought up with parents who loved me and supported me, I think it could have been different. But I didn't have that. And because I didn't have that, I wasn't used to it. I wasn't used to what love was.

'If you've been loved as a child,' she added, 'you recognise love when it comes along. You recognise what it means. I didn't. I didn't even know what love was, really.

'That makes a huge difference.'

The one love Dee had no trouble recognising was the love she felt for her son and the closeness they shared in those first years; while her husband was away on tour and before the outsiders made their way in and took over the stay-at-home role she wanted to fulfil herself.

'The best bits, the bits I loved the most were just after he was born,' she told me.

'I would give him his afternoon feed and change him, and then I'd get into bed with him and cuddle up. I really loved those times. I remember my mother-in-law saying I shouldn't do it because I could roll on him and smother him, but I knew I wouldn't.'

Dee knew because even when she was asleep, she was still half awake. Aware of having this warm little creature beside her, ready to tend to her baby's needs at a moment's notice.

'Those are the times I absolutely adored,' she said. 'I can remember bonding with him. I know for the first two days I was pretty out of it, because it had been a long labour, and on the third day, they put the cot beside the bed. I remember going over and pulling back the blanket, and just seeing him lying curled on his side, and there was this little damp patch under his bottom where he'd obviously leaked and I just felt this incredible rush of love.

'It was almost like something came out of my chest and joined with him. It was a physical feeling, this incredible feeling and this enormous sense of love, and feeling of love. And I just scooped him up and held him to me,' she said. 'It was just amazing.

'I wouldn't have missed that. I wouldn't have missed that for the world.

'But,' she added, 'I think for my son, bless him, I'm probably not the sort of mother he wanted, not the sort of mother he'd hoped he'd have.'

I wondered what sort of mum she thought he wanted. Dee wasn't sure.

'I don't know, really. I just think that possibly he would have wanted a mother more like his grandmother, his dad's mother. She was one of those people … I mean, she was extremely racist, very narrow-minded, but she could also be very charming. She was very light-hearted about things even though she had no compassion. She had no compassion for anyone. Neither did my son's dad.

'But I must admit, his mum loved my son and he adored her.

'You know, all we can do really as parents is raise our children to be able to make relationships,' she said. 'To hold down a job, to be able to make their way in the world safely. That's all we can do really. I don't think we can expect them to love us if they don't want to.

'I miss him,' she admitted, 'but I don't feel like I'm on my own. I mean, I'm too grown-up to feel that way, so it's a different type of loneliness. What I'm glad about is that he is obviously all right. He's got a job, he earns good money, they've got their own house, he is with a partner who he's been with for 12 years, so there must be something going right. I think it would be much worse if he'd committed suicide or been killed or something.

'He's still alive in the world and is doing okay, you know?

'The one thing I hope is that my son knows I love him. Which I know that he does.'

Once in a while they talk, but not often. Dee used to send him Christmas cards but never received any in return, so eventually she gave up. The closeness they felt in those early days may have changed, but she still loves him from a distance and is glad that he's happy.

Now her life and choices are her own. Now, finally, she puts herself first.

She still lives by the sea. But the once grand houses that populate her little town have been carved into more manageable slices of home. Sometimes the noise of gulls is lost to the constant, low-level hum of her neighbours playing computer games. Sometimes she thinks about writing again, but that low-level hum stops her.

Within the next year or so, she plans to fly to Switzerland, to a clinic that will help end her life and relieve her of the chronic pain she now feels in every inch of her body. I thought that maybe if her son knew, then that might bring them back together again. But then she told me that he already does: that she'd already explained her plans to him.

'He was a bit shocked,' she said, 'but he's just accepted it. He's just accepted it, and I think it's the best thing he could do, really, because if he got upset and asked me not to do it, that would have been much harder.'

Dee doesn't put herself last purely out of altruism, but also out of doubt. Out of a lack of confidence in herself; in her worth, and in her abilities. A lack of confidence, she says, that came from the lack of love she received as a child. That she never got to hear that she could do it, that she was special. All the things we need to hear as we try to find our place in the world.

'I just wish I'd had a mother of my own,' she told me. 'I wish I had a mum of my own, who would show me what to do.

'I regret that I didn't have parents, people who loved me.

'I regret very much that I wasn't more confident when I was younger.

'I spent a lot of my time as an adult trying to claim some confidence, trying to be more confident so that I could deal with things. And it's funny, I was just thinking about it on my birthday; how different my life might have been if I'd managed to conquer my fear. Because there was a lot of fear around when I was a child. I lived in an atmosphere of fear and I never really shook that off. Being afraid of doing things and afraid of trying things. Afraid of all sorts of things. Always afraid that I'd do something wrong or something would go wrong. And that,' she said, 'is still with me.

'However,' she added, 'I also have to accept that my upbringing was probably the cause of that. It wasn't something that I have failed to do or failed to learn; it was because of my particularly fragmented childhood that I ended up being a very nervous, withdrawn, shy, introverted child. Whereas, I think if I had had a different type of upbringing, I wouldn't have been quite so nervous and shy and introverted.

'Does that make sense?'

Not Fully Appreciating What You Have

KATIE

Katie Scarbrough was many things to many people. She was fun, and she was loyal. She was a champion ice skater in her youth. She had dark hair that skimmed her shoulders and a Northern Irish accent that had been tempered by years of living in England. She was happily married. The mother of eight-year-old Sam and four-year-old Sophie. And in 2012, she started writing a blog, charting her treatment for Stage 4 bowel cancer.

This chapter is very different from all the others. Because by the time I discovered Katie's blog, she had already died.

What you are about to read are her words, brought to you with the kind permission of her widow, Stuart. A few sentences have been trimmed, a few connecting words have been added for clarity, but the rest is resolutely her; of how she really felt as she faced an uncertain future and reflected on her past.

Katie's regrets weren't really about what she had or hadn't done during her life. They were about the things she hadn't fully appreciated and the things she was going to miss. Things we all tend to take for granted until it's too late: our health, the everyday, the privilege of becoming old and of being with the people we love.

'Today was always going to be a roller coaster of emotion,' she wrote.

And so it was. Because when I asked my opening question – what would you do if you only had one year to live? – it was Katie I was thinking about.

JULY, 2012
THE COUNTDOWN BEGINS

I am writing this and it's almost like I'm writing about another person.

When we walked into the Chemotherapy Unit I could feel the other patients' eyes on me, not only because I was new, but my age had a big impact. This became more apparent when a lovely woman who had been sitting a few chairs away with her husband came up to me and said, 'If you don't mind me asking, how old are you?' I replied 31, and she immediately replied, quite forcefully, 'You'll be fine … you'll be fine. My daughter was 31 when she was diagnosed and she is 34 now and she's fine, she had age on her side.'

The first drug was put through my vein over an hour and a half.

I started to feel numbness and tingling all the way up to my elbow, which I can still feel now. At least I managed to get two chapters read of *Fifty Shades of Grey*. All the nurses and patients kept coming over saying, 'OH, you have that book!!'

THE DAY AFTER THE TREATMENT

Waking up this morning, I felt a little scared to swallow. Having a psychological lump in my throat and taking tablets don't go together!! I had to start my 3rd Chemo drug this morning and they are bullet-sized. I've never been very good at taking big tablets and unfortunately these can't be cut. It took me a bit to get in the right frame of mind … that sounds so silly, but I think it was a mixture of how big they were and what they were.

After my mid-morning sickness blip I was hungry and ate a big bowl of Chicken Super Noodles with cheese, 2 slices of bread and a chocolate doughnut. Please don't slag off the Super Noodles until you try them. They are really yummy!!

THE PAST COUPLE OF WEEKS HAVE BEEN A BIT OF A BLUR...

One of my worst fears happened while I was in hospital. It was the dreaded moment Sam found out his mummy had the C word. Another child, slightly older, had obviously overheard an adult conversation and went and told him. So, Sam, out of the blue, asked Stuart if it was true.

This wasn't a word we wanted to use. We already told him that Mummy had a poorly belly and the doctors were giving me some medicine that was going to make me more poorly to begin with but make me better long-term. Both Stuart and I felt that was enough, for now, for a 7-year-old to take in, but had to respond truthfully and say that 'Yes, Mummy has Cancer of her tummy'. I'm still shocked by the whole thing!!

SEPTEMBER, 2012
AFTER CHEMO 4 AND 5

I know it's been a little while since my last blog but it's not because things have been bad. The last two weeks have been great. After chemo 4 I stayed in hospital for a couple of days to ensure the new anti-sickness drug worked. I was pleasantly surprised. I got back on my feet a lot quicker this time! I was so happy because it meant I could take Sophie to her first day at school. She looked so cute in her uniform. I handled it well until I came back home and looked at the pictures Stuart and I had taken. That's when I cried a little, not just because she's growing up so fast, but because I got to see that milestone!

At my consultation on Tuesday, my doctor ordered the scan for after my 6th chemo. That's going to be the next important step to aim for, as we will find out if my tumour has shrunk.

Thank you to everyone sending me their best wishes, it helps a lot to get through this!

ROLLER COASTER OF EMOTIONS

This week I have been a little emotional. It just seems like every time I turn on the TV or read a paper that the word Cancer is everywhere. It all started on Sunday while watching the Great North Run and seeing all the amazing people who are raising money for charities in people's memories. I think it's absolutely inspirational, but at the same time it sunk in that I'm one of those people that has this horrible illness.

OCTOBER, 2012
EVERYTHING IS CHANGING

How are you supposed to stop all the negative things from going through your head when every single minute I'm reminded of what I have?

As soon as I wake up I think 'Do I feel sick'? Then it hits me how uncomfortable I feel and the lack of energy I have. Just getting showered and dressed is a chore. I could easily sit and stare into space all day, every day. But, on the other side I have my kids and although they don't understand the real extent of what's going on, they are still going through it with me. They see their mum a little sadder than normal, with less energy than normal and frustrated that she can't do half the stuff she wants to. But the hugs and kisses I get from them both make everything that little bit brighter.

ONE BIG NIGHTMARE!!

I've been sitting here wondering how I am supposed to put what I'm about to say into words, but there is no easy way. Some people may think it's inappropriate, but I don't really care as I have nothing to hide and nothing to be ashamed of.

Yesterday, Stuart and I went to the hospital to get the results of the CT scan I had a week ago. Deep down I knew it wasn't going to be good news. You can try and be as positive as possible but deep down you have to listen to how your body is feeling. My consultant took us into her room with my Oncology Nurse and told us that my tumours have become more dense and my ovaries more enlarged. The chemotherapy I have been having to tackle Bowel Cancer hasn't worked. We were given two options: do nothing and I would have 6 months (apparently this is something they have to offer in case you don't feel up to more chemo) or try a chemotherapy which targets the ovaries. I have no option but to try the chemotherapy.

Needless to say, our whole family are devastated. I am angry that it has come to this, but we have to keep the fight going.

SIT BACK AND WAIT FOR THE FALLOUT

This probably sounds so silly, but for me the hardest thing to deal with is that my hair is going to fall out. I can deal with the tiredness, sickness (to some extent) and the redness of the hands and feet, but the loss of my hair scares me. It's probably because I'm unsure how the kids will react, more so Sam. I don't want his friends to say horrible things about me to him. I'm not saying they will, but this is the stuff I worry about.

NOVEMBER, 2012
FAMILY TIME!!

At the end of my last blog I said how we were going to Disney On Ice. Well, we went and it was great, the kids really enjoyed it. Sophie was in her element dressed in her Minnie Mouse costume. Sam was a little held back, but loved it too.

Two days later we went to Belfast. Sam always hates the drive up to Cairnryan as it takes 5 hrs, then 2 hrs on the boat. But we got there without too many 'Are we there yets?' The one person I wanted to see most of all was my 98-year-old Nana. It was a bit emotional seeing her, for the both of us, to be honest. I also had a catch-up with friends that I used to ice skate with, rep with in Majorca and go to school with. I know there were a lot of people that wanted to catch up with me and I'm sorry I wasn't able to.

My hair also started to fall out. Each day I woke up and had a shower there was more and more on my pillow and in the bath. I was crying and Sophie came up to me and hugged me and said, 'Don't worry Mummy, if your hair falls out tomorrow and you're sad, call me, okay?' She's such a cutie pie. On the way back, as we were sailing down Belfast Lough, it hit me that this could have been the last time I'm ever here. That got me upset.

On Sunday morning more of my hair had fallen out. I couldn't take waking up every morning to the hair on my pillow so I made the decision to shave it. I haven't gone completely mad, but had a number three all over. I'm

REGRETS OF THE DYING

finding it a lot better to deal with and may opt for a zero at some point.

THE WEEK BEFORE DISNEY...

Is it weird that every time I watch TV and see someone with beautiful hair that I get jealous?

Is it weird that I get jealous of my own husband playing with the kids as I want to do the same but don't have the energy? Then I watch the soaps on telly and listen to their pathetic storylines which aren't real but what is happening to me IS real and that makes me feel mad!! Everywhere I look I'm reminded that I am a 'Cancer Patient' and there is no getting away from it. Sometimes I just feel like screaming why me?!

I haven't done anything wrong to deserve this.

My hair is more or less completely out now and I find it such a struggle just to get in the shower, as I don't want to look at it. I haven't been feeling particularly great since last week's chemo, but that has only come in the past few days. It's not that I have been sick but I'm feeling queasy, tired and some of my joints have been hurting. I know when I'm feeling better I can do more things, but when I'm not feeling right everything gets on top of me. I also know I need to snap out of this as we are going to Disneyland Paris and that needs to be great for the kids!! We haven't told them yet so it's a complete surprise!! I can't wait to see their faces.

DECEMBER, 2012
IT'S THE MOST WONDERFUL TIME OF THE YEAR!

We've been back from Disneyland for a few weeks now and it's been pretty hectic. We had a magical time in Paris. The kids had a great time going on the rides, meeting the different characters, seeing the shows and parades. It is definitely something that has brought us amazing memories which will last forever. I'm sure other parents will agree, to see your children smiling and happy is the best feeling in the world. It was a little bubble of magic that got burst pretty quick when you get home and realise your reality.

Christmas is not far away now and you don't realise how grateful I am for my laptop. The thought of walking around the shops when it's busy is enough to pull my hair out … if I had any, lol.

Sophie had her first 'Nativity Play' at primary school this week. I have to say I am one proud mummy. She only told me the night before that she was Mary. And because she hadn't said anything before, I wasn't sure if she may have gotten it wrong so I tried not to get too excited about it, but while we were waiting to go into the classroom, I looked through the window in the door and there she was, dressed as Mary. She looked so cute. When I got diagnosed with Cancer back in June, one thought that had gone through my head was the fact that Sophie was starting Primary School and I wanted to see her in the

Nativity. The fact she was Mary and I got to see her was the icing on the cake!!

JANUARY, 2013

TWAS THE SEASON TO BE... SICK!!

I had built Christmas up to be a day where I was going to feel great, have a few drinks, enjoy spending time with my family and watch the kids play with their new toys. I wanted it to be the best ever Christmas!! However, for me it didn't match up to my expectations.

Around Christmas Eve I started feeling queasy. My tummy had gotten bigger and harder, I wasn't able to eat the amount I wanted to and I had a metallic taste in my mouth. It's funny, on Christmas morning Sam wouldn't come downstairs without one of us going with him as he thought Santa was still there. Down the stairs we went and the first thing Sam noticed was Sophie's new bike. She was so excited, sitting on it with a big smile. Sam opened his biggest present and it was a new scooter he had asked for, so he was happy too. Sophie was in her element when she found her Jessie costume (from *Toy Story*), she immediately put it on. That for me was the best part, and to be honest, I was feeling sick at the time but made myself push through it, as I didn't want my sickness to ruin the day. As I was feeling low anyway, I couldn't help but think that that could be the last time I see them opening presents at Christmas.

That now brings me to my scan results.

Stuart and I took his parents to the hospital yesterday for support. I knew that in the past two weeks my health has gotten that little bit worse. But I was able to breathe my tummy in, which I hadn't been able to do before. So, without saying too much out loud, I thought the chemo may be working. But the doctor told us that the tumour on my liver has gotten bigger and the cancer has now spread to two points in my bones on my back. The tumour in my bowel is stable. She did explain why I have been feeling the way I have: that everything had been pushing on my liver, which is also why I have the metallic taste in my mouth and the sickness.

After hearing this, I had a massive lump in my throat and I knew if I started crying I wouldn't be able to hold it together.

This is the first time I have been able to talk about yesterday ... well, just about. I have to say this blog has been a struggle. I can't even talk to my mum and dad about it yet (sorry, Mum and Dad) because I'd end up breaking down into tears and I am trying to hold that back as crying makes me feel more queasy.

I can only say I feel numb at the minute. I do know that when cancer gets in the bones, that really isn't a good sign and it's hard to get back from there. I keep wishing that Damon and Stefan from *The Vampire Diaries* would come and feed me their blood, then kill me and I would become an immortal. Or Edward and Carlisle would come and bite me with their venom!! That way I know I would be around for a really long time.

Thank you everyone who has been keeping up to date with my journey so far. This is not me giving up, this is just me trying to come to terms with what I have been told.

xxxxx

PS Sorry if this gets any of you upset, I probably should have put a warning at the beginning.

TIME IS NOT JUST A SCALE...

It's hard to put into words and explain how much cancer takes over EVERYTHING!! Not only in me, my family, my friends and even people I don't know. It's a S**T disease and I can say the novelty of having it has well and truly worn off!!

I get up in the morning and it's there, I talk to Stuart and it's there, I look at the kids and it's there, I watch TV and it's there, and I go to bed and it's there. I can hear it in people's voices and see it in their eyes. There is no way of getting away from it.

The worst thing is looking in the mirror and seeing what it has done to me. I don't recognise me anymore, I look like a typical cancer patient, skinny, bald and anorexic-looking. I'd give anything to go back to the girl I was, even though I didn't like my appearance much then, it's way better than what I am now. It's the nature of the beast that grows inside of me, of which I have no control!!

This week has been very hard and emotional on everyone. I can't say that this week is the hardest ever because every week seems to be the hardest ever.

Anyway, I went into hospital on Monday as my tummy was so painful and distended. The amount of fluid that had built up was so immense that I was struggling to take a deep breath and the smallest amount of food was making me sick.

On Tuesday, I was given a very strong anti-sickness medication which made me very drowsy. When my doctor and nurse came into the room I saw four people and not two. It was very strange and I didn't really like it. That evening the bowel surgeon, a palliative care manager and a nurse came into my room. I was a little more with it by then and all I kept thinking is their mannerisms were all very morbid. He told me that my Cancer was very aggressive (which we already knew) and that it was causing the fluid to build up on my tummy (again, we already knew this). Due to how the atmosphere felt in the room and the looks on their faces, I felt I was running out of time to ask questions.

I asked about operating and they said that wouldn't benefit me as it would take six weeks to recover from surgery before any other Chemotherapy could be given. I then proceeded to ask the question about time scales. He told me in a low morbid voice that it could be weeks if nothing works!! WOW, how am I supposed to take that in? It felt like someone had punched me in the chest and taken my heart out. It all made sense why they were all there and why it felt so morbid.

Weeks, weeks, weeks. That could mean I have as little as a week left, or as long as 52 weeks.

I'm angry and upset, as I don't know what I have done to deserve this. I must have done something unforgivable and I would do ANYTHING to make it right. Time is precious and that's what gets me, not knowing if things like birthdays are reachable.

FEBRUARY, 2013
WHAT A HECTIC WEEK!!!

Since my last blog, I have managed to pick myself up, dust myself down and gain a little bit more perspective and clarity on things. I think I needed to have a complete meltdown to bring me out the other side. To be honest, it is good to have a good cry!!

Using Twitter this week has made me want to use it to help spread the word about such a horrible disease. I have been in the situation where a doctor takes one look at you and says, 'You are only 31, I think it's a red herring, if it's anything else I will eat my hat.' And now look at the position I'm in. Doctors need to stop using statistics so much and realise Cancer can happen to anyone at any age. This isn't to scaremonger anyone but if you have any symptoms, go to your doctor and get them checked out. It may be nothing but the earlier a potential problem is found, the earlier it can be treated.

I keep thinking back to 'The Hospital Room' moment I had a few weeks ago and question, did it really happen? It almost feels like a bad dream, which is probably a good thing. But then on the other hand, am I in denial about it, even though I go over in my head that my Cancer is terminal and inoperable? I don't know where I have found the strength to do everything I am doing right now. When I was younger, I wouldn't say boo to anyone. I even remember crying in Primary School when I was moved to sit next to a boy!! I would wear my heart on my sleeve, worry about everything and what people thought of me. I thought I would be handling this in such a different way, I have actually started to amaze myself!!

xxx

PS Did you know in the space of three and a half weeks I have had 14 litres of fluid drained from my tummy!! Which is 7 two-litre bottles of Pepsi Max. How mad is that?

LONDON BABY!!

We only decided to go to London after Stuart stemmed a question to me, 'What do you want to do for your birthday?' So, I said go to London to sightsee and maybe see a show.

The satnav took us straight through the centre. We went past Harrods, which was all lit up, The Ritz, Leicester Square and Piccadilly Circus. The kids were very excited but tired after their long day. At the hotel we got our PJs on and climbed into bed with drinks, Pringles and watched WWE on TV. The kids were soon fast asleep.

On Sunday morning, it was the first time since we arrived in London that I had thought about having Cancer.

Sam and I were watching TV while getting dressed and the new Macmillan Cancer Support advert came on, the one with the people falling over and how many people get diagnosed each day. Sam was glued to it, and after I asked him what it made him think of. He said, 'You, with Cancer in a grave.' My heart jumped into my mouth. I tried to hold it together and gave him a huge hug. I had to go into the bathroom to tell Stuart, cry a little and compose myself. That was a hard thing to hear. When I came out, he was happily playing.

We had planned to go home straight from the hotel on the Monday, but because we hadn't been to M&M World, we decided to go there first. I've never seen so much merchandise. Needless to say, we bought quite a bit, so we have a stack of mementos!! I wanted to buy the brown cushions with the faces on, but they were a little too expensive ... maybe next time.

WHAT A DIFFERENCE A WEEK MAKES
MARCH, 2013

This time last week I had energy. I was eating, drinking and moving around. What I'm doing now is sitting in a hospital on IV drugs. It's a big turnaround in comparison.

Stuart called the chemo ward to ask them about me starting on my antibiotics and to tell them about the cramps and sickness. I had an X-ray, then on Wednesday we were told the X-ray didn't show a lot, so I was booked for a CT scan. It was difficult having the scan done, due to my tummy and how sitting up straight made me sick. If I eat or drink it just sits in my chest as there is no room in my tummy with all my organs pressing together, so I haven't really eaten since Saturday. That night I sat and watched *Child of Our Time* on BBC1. It follows 25 kids born in the millennium, who have now reached their teens. This made me think of Sam and Sophie, and it got me upset as I was trying to imagine them as teenagers and how much they will change. I can't imagine I will get to see it and that's tough to get my head round.

That brings us to yesterday and what another bad news day it was!! My Bowel Surgeon, Oncologist and Clinical Nurse Specialist came in with the results of my scan. The tumours look more dense on my bowel and liver, hence why my tummy has gotten big again. It was one of those death-sentence moments. My head was spinning. I asked the surgeon to operate, as at least doing something was better than doing nothing. His response was that it was too risky and I would have a 6-week recovery time before any chemo could be given. My response was (with tears flowing down my face), 'Why can't you at least open me up and have a look and maybe my ovaries could be removed to give me more room in my tummy?' I just keep thinking I need more room to eat because if I can't eat then it's all downhill from there. I was screaming inside!! He said, 'But I could open you up and you could end up with an infection and things could look worse than the scan shows.'

Everything came across negative and not positive at all. I felt deflated and low, and all the things that have kept me going over the last few weeks didn't seem to matter anymore. I just want them to do something as that's better than not doing anything at all!!

I am trying to weigh it up and part of me is even thinking that, surely, it's better to die fighting on an operating table rather than just waiting for the cancer to take hold even more than it already has. This is exactly where we are at now … no more options!!

I have lost a lot of weight. My legs are weak and I struggle to climb the stairs. I feel like a 70-year-old!! Cancer has taken everything away from me and I hate it!! I hate that it's making me bitter and emotional. I hate that it's given me no hope, I hate that it's made me weak and dependent and, most of all, I hate that it's going to take me away from my kids and family!!!

DOING NOTHING IS NOT AN OPTION!!

A few weeks ago, after asking my Oncologist to send my biopsy to Harley Street, she came to see me. I was having chemo at the time and she said that I couldn't keep using up my energy running up and down the country looking for answers when I will be told the same thing everywhere I go. I was so upset and started crying and told her that I can't just do nothing, and that every time I come into hospital for scan results, etc. I keep getting told negative information and that doesn't help me stay positive. I said

I am only 32 and have two kids and I need to do all that's possible for them. She thinks I should go home and enjoy the rest of my time with my family. But I don't want my kids to see me waste away. I also want them to know their mummy fought this to the end and didn't give up!!! I would still rather die on an operating table than die somewhere like a hospice, as I know at some point I wouldn't want the kids to see me in any kind of fragile state. And not seeing them would be completely heart-breaking.

I am not in denial; I know I have Stage 4 cancer and it's inoperable but I need to have the HOPE that maybe there is something more, and if I don't at least try, what kind of impression does that send to my kids?

I watched *Child of Our Time* again last night and I wish I hadn't. One of the girls lost her mum when she was 8 years old. Ironically enough her surname was the same as ours. Again, I was in floods of tears. I felt it was a sign.

APRIL, 2013
HITTING A BRICK WALL

On Sunday, after watching *Jurassic Park* with the kids, we decided it was time to tell them something. We have said all along we don't want to lie to them. We told them that Mummy's medicine isn't working anymore and there isn't anything the doctors can do for me. Sam looked at me and I asked him what that made him think, he said that you're going to die. I said yes. Stuart, Sam and I burst into tears.

That was the hardest thing I have EVER had to do.

Sophie was bouncing around the room. I explained to Sam that Sophie doesn't understand as she's so young. He then explained to her, saying Mummy's Calpol medicine isn't working. She came over and said she didn't want me to die.

We had an Oncologist appointment for Tuesday (yesterday) and knew it wasn't going to be good news. She reiterated the fact that the cancer was stable on the peritoneal and ovaries but had grown on the liver and bones. I asked to get my tummy drained as the fluid had built up and I was very uncomfortable, which she organised.

The fluid build-up is another sign that the medicine isn't working.

I asked how long it would take for my liver to give up and she said a few weeks.

My doctor said there wasn't anything more that they could do and I knew that in my head, but it's hard to hear. Now it's all about symptom control. I am not in a great way. My head is strong but my body is giving up. My back is sore, my lower left-hand side where my liver is, is sore, and today my eyes have started to go yellow. I am also very thin and can only eat small amounts of food.

I think at this point I am in denial about what is going to happen. I really don't know how to die, does anybody? Stuart and I are numb, devastated and trying to keep things normal for the kids. But this is very far from a 'normal' situation.

I had booked a birthday party for Sophie but had to cancel it today.

It is too late to think of a 'Bucket List' but I want to go to the beach on the South Coast and feel the wind on my face and watch the kids play on the sand.

It's really difficult to explain how I feel. I am angry, confused and teary, and find myself staring into space all the time not really thinking of anything.

You don't think when you have kids that you won't see it through and see them grow up into adults, and this is what's hard to take in more than anything. The fact is I won't see what type of man Sam will grow into and what type of woman Sophie will grow up to be, what job they will have, who they will marry, get to know my grandkids, be there on their wedding days and generally be their mum, as they so need a mum. And that's supposed to be my job!!!

All I want to do is see my kids grow up and grow old with my husband!!

I want to say thank you to everyone who has read my blog, commented, and donated money.

You are all amazeballs!!

That was Katie's last blog. She died eight days later, at the age of 32.

One year she was alive and seemingly well, and the next she was gone.

When she knew her time was running out, her focus wasn't about bucket lists and grand plans, it was about watching her two children play and trying to make it to Christmas. She was never happy with the way she looked, but near the end she came to realise how pretty she was, and how strong and healthy her body had already been; she found out how outspoken she could be, now that she had something to really fight for. And when she became unable to do the school run, or pop to the shops, or even play with her kids, she rediscovered how important those moments were, too.

The things that fill our days. The important stuff.

Katie knew they were important. They were woven into everything she wrote in those final months, her words steeped in an undeniable love for all she was going to leave behind.

Regrets That Change With Time

COLIN

About 30 years ago I asked Colin what his biggest regret was. His answer was having children. This will be a short but personal chapter, because Colin is my dad.

Since asking him that question many things have changed. He's now a non-drinking alcoholic, rather than a drinking one; he is, at the age of 73, quite a bit older; he's also had both kidney and prostate cancer, has survived being put into an induced coma and has been diagnosed with chronic obstructive pulmonary disease.

His day-to-day life has completely changed, along with his outlook.

He knew I was writing this book, so we started talking about the things he personally wished he had or hadn't done over the years. Deep down, the reason I kept bringing the subject up was because of that moment three decades ago when his answer was 'having children'.

Would his answer be the same now? Or would it have changed?

So, I asked him again: 'What is your biggest regret?'

When I originally posed that question as a 15-year-old teenager his reaction was clear and definite, but now it wasn't. In fact, he changed his answer about five or six times throughout our conversation: from his work not being as successful as it could have been, to some random woman he'd had an affair with; to his drinking, and him generally not being around when his family needed him. So, I wrote him a letter instead, something that would allow him some time and space to read and digest what I was asking before he replied.

I opened with: 'Dear Dad, I'm sorry I keep asking you this …' then replayed what he had told me all those years before, adding that this was what I was trying to ask him during our recent conversation but couldn't quite find the words.

About a week later, he replied via text. Reproduced with his permission, this is what he said:

Hiya Georgy, received your letter today!

I wish you'd mentioned your upset about my weird comment as a child?

The one thing in my life that keeps me going is my children! and now grandchild.

I must have been very depressed at the time but would never think I've missed any opportunities because of you? Just my own failings, ha!

I will put pen to paper about Lynette, the woman who changed my life for the worse … always love you, Georgy.

Your dad xxx

The moment I hadn't been able to forget, he couldn't actually remember.

Deep down, I think (I know) he did regret having us back then: we got in the way, we gave him more responsibilities and financial pressure than his chaotic upbringing could have prepared him for. But then isn't now. Now, he may have other regrets, but the main one is no longer me. Hopefully none of them are.

Dad kept promising to send me that letter, but it never came. Maybe that regret had dissipated, too.

Part Three

LOVE

'Never love anyone who treats
you like you're ordinary.'

— *Oscar Wilde* —

Losing the Love of Your Life

SID

The first thing he showed me was a photograph. He's pictured standing. She's beside him, smiling at the camera; wearing his cardigan. It was 1969 and Sid and Lilias were in love. Today, his feelings remain unchanged even though they haven't spoken for over 50 years.

Sid is 73 now and in the process of trying to get his life 'in order before,' he says 'it's too late.' He has lived without Lilias for over five decades and he wants to make amends. For missing all that time and for the way it ended.

We met at his nearest train station, a brass-tipped walking stick keeping him steady as we found each other among the stream of travellers. Later, I would realise how apt this location would be for our first encounter, but at the time my focus was drawn to his neat white beard, his novelty tie (a fish being caught on a line) and to his dark grey suit that fell a bit baggy – he told me that he'd lost weight over the last few years, mainly due to the two lung conditions he had: asbestosis, a disease caused by inhaling asbestos fibres, and a shadow he'd developed during his life spent as a deep-sea diver.

We walked outside to his car and I headed for the passenger seat, while Sid walked towards the boot. He popped it open, pulled out a photo album and started flicking through the pages. 'This was her,' he said, showing me that picture of them both. Pointing to a slim, attractive woman with straight dark hair; wanting me to have a point of reference to the regret we were going to discuss. And then we set off. Through the suburbs and towards his white semi-detached cottage. A quiet corner of the world; a vegetable patch to the side.

Sid and Lilias's story started once upon a time in Lincolnshire. Their meeting was a very simple one: he spotted her across the street, crossed the road and asked her out.

'I saw Lilias with her friend, and I don't know why, but I walked up to her and introduced myself and asked would it be possible to meet up later on, in the evening. And the answer, was yes.'

They were both about 20 at the time and were both away from home: he was working on a construction site, yet to start his career as a diver; she was staying in a holiday camp with a friend (think the Catskills in *Dirty Dancing*, without the watermelons and brisket). Later on, the friend would comment, 'Aren't Englishmen bold?' But Sid didn't usually go up to strangers in the street and ask them out. That was the first time he did it, and the last.

I asked what compelled him to cross that road.

'I'd never have met her otherwise, would I? There was just something there, there was just something. I walked straight across the road and said, "Excuse me."'

He described her as beautiful, very well-spoken, very pleasant. From Scotland. An educated woman with nice legs. A librarian who would write dates on everything, cataloguing their existence and place. 'She was genuinely lovely,' he said, then added, 'and I mean that.'

But not everyone in his family agreed. 'My sister took to her, my mum did, my father did for a time. I don't think anybody ever said anything bad about her as such, but then perhaps that was young love, not listening. I don't know.'

He flipped open his photo album again and pointed to an image of them both: 'Look, both wearing slippers.'

That first date was spent having a few drinks and going ice skating, her friend acting as chaperone. He laughed, thinking back to that night and how he could hardly walk the next day, his calves hurt so much. And then as they were getting closer, he started his new, more dangerous job underwater. He travelled to oilfields in the Middle East, Norway, Nigeria – wherever there was salvage or recovery work to be done – turning their love into a long-distance affair as he made his way around the world and she stayed at home, back in Scotland. But they managed to keep it together. Using phone calls and posting letters, back and forth, keeping the communication going between face-to-face meets when they would reunite at various train stations across England, Scotland and Wales on his visits home.

'I used to arrange for Lilias to be at a phone box,' he explained. 'I used to phone her on certain nights at certain times and the writing was obviously everything. So, we kept in touch even though we were stretched far apart.'

Life went on like this for about two and a half years. Them writing to each other and calling on various payphones. Them meeting up. Him travelling around and her staying put.

'But unfortunately,' he added, 'it all went very wrong. We actually … I'd actually got us a flat. We were going to set up home. I got the keys. Most of the knives, forks and bedding were organised. And then I got posted away again.'

There were no arguments or goodbyes. He'd been away before but this time, for some reason, he let their correspondence slide. And then it was over.

I wondered what happened to their flat.

'I had to pay for a month's rent and that was it.'

And what about all those knives, forks and bedding that he had bought, what happened to them? He said he didn't know. He presumed they were 'probably left for the next lot. It was all still wrapped up and clean'.

'So, you never got to live there with her?' I asked.

'I never got to see her again,' he replied.

Listening to Sid relay what happened, it was quite hard to understand how he could walk away from someone he loved so much. But back then, in the 60s and 70s, life wasn't always as swinging as some of the history books would have us believe. Most people still lived their lives through the gaze of social propriety: people had sex before marriage, they just pretended they didn't; they had babies without a permanent partner, they just told a few lies to cover it up or were shuttled off to give birth in secret.

I remembered what Sid had said about his dad liking Lilias 'for a time'. Was his disapproval the reason they didn't move in together?

'I don't think father was too happy with the situation,' he admits. 'He expressed that what we wanted to happen was not going to happen. He said, basically, that he wasn't very impressed with the idea of having grandchildren born out of wedlock. Well, I don't know what to say about that. We hadn't got as far as having any. In the meantime, I got a posting elsewhere. And of course, it never happened at all then. That got nipped in the bud.'

He never got the chance to tell Lilias what happened; that his dad didn't approve and so he couldn't go through with it. He said he was away in Nigeria, working. He was, as usual, away for three, four, five months at a go. And because he kept moving about, their communication became broken.

The last time they saw each other was like all the others. It wasn't a *Brief Encounter* moment, it just happened to be the final goodbye, even though they didn't know it at the time.

'I remember putting her on a train back to Aberdeen. I turned my back and walked away and the next letter I got from her said, "I was looking out of the window and you never looked back." It broke my heart.'

I asked what his last words to her were. For a moment so clearly embedded in his memory, he was unsure. 'Goodbye?'

he said. 'Goodbye, see you? Or take care, maybe? It was never … we hadn't parted at that time, there was going to be another tomorrow.'

What Sid didn't know was that Lilias had been writing to him, care of his father's house – the only address she had. She sent letters that told him about her marriage to another man, and about having a baby. But Sid never received them. In fact, he knew nothing about them until his father died and they were found among his personal effects.

'The letters were still coming, but it wasn't until we cleared his house that we found a few more that suggested that she was, for a little while anyway, still writing. And by the time I got them, I'd totally lost her. I was torn a bit there, because as I say, my dad was …'

Sid trailed off, leaving his sentence unfinished.

When I asked him if he was angry with his father for not approving of their union, for keeping her letters hidden, he said no. He seemed to understand that a man born in 1917, who spent his life in the military, was also a loving father who could maybe see the future clearer than Sid could at the age of 21.

'He was a lovely chap, my father,' he said. 'A proper leader of men. And he could probably see something in there that I didn't. He never talked about it but he put his foot down.'

Sid still has the picture that Lilias sent him housed safely away in his album: of her daughter laying on a green coloured settee. 'It said, "This is Gaynor aged 11 weeks, a lot bigger now, love Lilias".' A date marked on the back, the moment catalogued as always. The father, the man she ended up marrying, was a red-headed motor mechanic – and the brother of the friend who chaperoned them on their first date all those years before.

Sid never fell in love again. He never had children, or grandchildren. He went out with people, he worked and had adventures, but love would stay boxed into those two and a half years of arranged calls to phone boxes, letters and train stations.

'Unfortunately,' he said, 'you can't really have much of a relationship if you're carrying that around with you, can you? Don't get me wrong, I've had acquaintances but I never met anyone else I considered to be of any value.

'I've got to bury my ghosts. She's here, she's there, but not in any physical state.

'I do miss that somebody to look forward to and someone to smile at when they come downstairs, or someone to listen to me. The warmth of actually having another human being in the house. But it was my own ... I didn't want to put anyone else through that.'

So, Sid keeps his ghosts neatly filed away in his photo albums.

I asked him why he'd kept hold of them for all these years.

'Because I can't let go,' he admitted. 'I just can't. I've still got the originals upstairs in a biscuit tin full of money. All foreign currencies, of course.'

'Are you lonely?' I asked.

'Yes,' he replied. 'I am the loneliest person on this earth.'

I spoke to him in the middle of the pandemic. The pubs he would usually go to for chats and company were all operating strict systems: where you were sat down at a table and served at that table, and you entered via one door and exited via another. The two-metre rule proved to be a hard distance to surmount for those living alone and looking for some community.

'The world has changed. I've got no chance of having a social life now. I've been doing my front garden up, with wall-flowers and sweet williams, so I get neighbours walking past and people walking dogs who will chat. That's about the only time I ever talk to anybody now.'

His world used to be a huge and varied thing. It used to be thousands of miles wide and hundreds of metres deep. Now, it is not.

'I look forward to the post,' he told me. 'Even if it's only a bill. Something through the door to say, "you're still here".'

Sid had led such a nomadic life. He admits, even when he worked in the UK, he never went home on a Friday night like the rest of the lads, he just didn't feel the need. I wondered if there was a reason why he found it so hard to settle down: an explanation as to why he found making long-term commit-ments tricky. At first, he put it down to 'the wanderlust of the Irish', inherited from his mother's side. But then I remem-bered about his dad being in the Armed Forces and him being sent away to boarding school at the age of 10. He denied that that had had an effect on him, that he didn't go home because home was just too far away, but added: 'You take it in your stride. But you've got to understand, for children of the RAF you made friends with the people on the camp and then their dads got posted away, so you didn't really have ... I don't have any long-term friendships at all.'

So, work was his focus for most of his life. And now, he is one of the last men standing. He used to have hundreds of colleagues, but he noted, indicating the size of his living room, 'If we had a reunion now, we'd probably all fit in here.'

Sid realised his career had come to an end when he found himself double-guessing what he was doing and how safe he was, in a way that he never had before. So, he retired and decorated his home with the trinkets and mementos he'd gathered over the years: a brass diving helmet placed in an unused fireplace, a stuffed fish fixed to the wall. More photos, more albums.

When Sid and Lilias first met, he moved from working on a building site at home to something high-risk and high-reward far away. I wondered, if he had changed his line of work back then, whether that would have made a difference? Whether, maybe, they'd still be together? At first, Sid said, 'Probably, yes.' But then, later on, after he'd had a chance to ponder on it for a couple of weeks, we talked again about this idea of making a different choice and his view had changed slightly, maybe towards the more realistic end of the 'what if...?' scenario: 'I think a young man has got to get that out, you've got to get that stupidity out of you. We used to lose more divers jumping out of mistresses' bedroom windows than we ever did at sea. It was the lifestyle, the fast cars, the booze.'

He had mentioned the risks and rewards, but that wasn't why he did what he did, or what had kept him there for so long. 'I think it was just the adrenaline,' he said. 'For some reason, I could cope very, very well with dark, dirty water and confined spaces.'

Sid tried to get me to imagine how deep 'deep' was. That the deepest he ever went was 770 feet. That's eight times as tall as Big Ben, or three times the height of the Taj Mahal.

He explained how, when they would rise back up to the surface, they would have to take a certain amount of time to do it or the water pressure could cause tissue and nerve damage, even death. He also pointed out that it took them, relatively, more time to return to the water's surface than astronauts returning back to earth. That seemed pretty deep. I think most of us, trapped in a confined space, weighed down by layers and layers of heavy clothing and equipment, would feel claustrophobic. Panicked, even.

Sid smiled, and said if you do that 'you're dead'.

He broke off for a minute and then continued, returning to my original question about the possibility of changing jobs so he could stay close to home.

'There is no answer, is there?' he said. '"If only" is really 20/20 vision, isn't it? Hindsight. Oh, if only I'd have done this, if only I had done that ... Ifs are no good to me, are they? No good to anyone.'

In reality, as much as he loved her, it was obvious he loved his work too. He was drawn to it, just as he had been drawn to her, and it became part of him.

'It could have gone the other way, because at one time I could have got myself transferred up to the oilfields in Aberdeen, but if we'd just been down here, she would have got lonely and homesick. Or maybe she could have come travelling with me. I don't know. I just— I'm pleased I did it, let's put it like that. But,' he added, 'I just wish, now, that that had turned out different for both of us. But, the whole thing … I really did love that woman, but it's all over and done with, is it not?'

I thought about what love is and what it means to us. To Sid, it meant this: 'It's the trust and listening for the car engine coming home. Sitting down and having your evening meal together. It's that joining of two human beings who want to be together, who want to— Oh crikey, I'm going to break down here …'

He composed himself and then carried on: 'Any relationship has got to mesh in like a set of cogs. Because when you get it right, the cogs fit. It's not all going to be roses, but sharing the bad things is as good as sharing the good things. If it's right, your heart misses a beat when you see them. But that's all gone, isn't it? That's all gone.

'Why is it in the makeup of a human being that they select one person over another?' he pondered. 'Why did I walk up to a perfect stranger?'

'Do you still love her?' I asked.

'Oh yes, yes, yes, yes,' he replied.

'Do you think you would have gotten married?'

'Yes. Yes, it would have been in church.'

Fifty years on and his answer was still yes.

They had only spent about two and a half years together, mostly speaking from a great distance, and his answer was still yes.

'It was absolute sheer bliss, all the time,' he admitted. 'I don't think we ever had a discussion on anything that required a bit of confrontation at all. It seemed to me that that was going to be it, forever and ever, imagining things being nice and sharing things and sitting at the table together. Then of course that all got blown out of the water, didn't it?'

While there are a few reminders of their time together dotted around his home, it hadn't become a shrine to her. Her pictures are carefully put away, there's a pewter mug with, 'Happy 21st, love, Lilias' inscribed on it and a few books she'd given to him. Every time Sid went away to another far-flung part of the globe, he would buy her a little doll dressed in that country's national costume. She collected them, like he collected his photos.

I wondered if she had kept hers safe and sound, too.

A few months before Sid and I met, he flew up to Scotland to see if he could find her. He went back to the only address he had and enquired if the new owners knew where the old owners might be. They didn't. They didn't know any of the names he offered, or recognise any of the people he described. Sid knew it was a long shot. Lilias would be in her 70s, her husband a few years older – there was no guarantee either of them would still be alive.

Then a local newspaper found out about Sid's quest and covered his story, including Sid's wish to name Lilias as his sole beneficiary when he dies, and put out a request asking for anyone with information to get in contact. At first, there were calls from well-wishers, urging him to keep looking, but no real leads; then came a few offers of marriage from women hoping to secure that inheritance he had on offer.

For a while, he lost faith. And then a family member got in contact: Lilias's daughter, the little baby who was once photographed on that green sofa many years ago. Their message to Sid was short and simple: 'She wants no contact with you.'

Lilias didn't want his money, or his letters. Or to give him another, more recent photo. Her life had moved on. She had married another man and they had a child. And her life did not have room for Sid in it, or his requests for more. He had hit a dead end. But even now, there were moments when he still talked with hope and in a way, denial.

'The family don't want to know anything about me,' he said. 'I can understand. If you think about it, this bloke has turned up out of the blue, after 50 years ... But I hate the idea of lying in my grave thinking, I should have done that.'

So, why didn't he fight for her when he had the chance?

Why didn't he reconnect the moment he returned from Nigeria?

'I don't know,' he admitted. 'I just drifted away.

'I shouldn't have left it like that, but that's 20/20 vision, hindsight, is it not? I don't know if we'd even speak the same language now. It probably wouldn't have worked. I'd certainly have had to pack up being away because I couldn't think of anything worse than taking a little lass out of her culture, her family, her friends.

'I certainly would not have taken her abroad. So, there you go.'

When Lilias's family declined his wish to resume contact, it also left him with the question: Where will his house, assets and 'things' go when he dies?

'When this' – he gestured to himself – 'goes, that's it. It's the end of the line, it's finished and I'd rather it went to someone that thought something of me at one point.'

If she couldn't have it, then he didn't seem to be bothered where it went. Like it was just another point of practicality: 'I won't be there, will I?' he stated.

If he had had children, then his problem would have been solved. He wanted them, but it just never happened. He confessed that when he found those lost letters and saw that picture of Lilias's daughter, his overriding feeling was 'Look what you would have won.' That here is the life that could have been his.

'I think there'd be nothing nicer than to be a grandad now.'

He nodded towards a box room located off his lounge, to a train set inherited from his own father: 'I don't know who to give it to,' he said. So, it sits, unused but ever-ready.

'I would dearly like to meet that lass again. I'd love to, and this is something I have thought about: I just want to put it right, if I can. Bury my ghosts. But I can't turn the clock back unfortunately. It's never going to happen. I would have loved if I could have got a photograph of her taken in the last 10 years, just to tidy the whole thing up. But that's not going to happen either. You only get one run, don't you?

'It could have really been something,' he added, 'but I never put down the roots.'

As I was leaving, Sid opened up one of the books Lilias had given him, a *Roadmap of Great Britain*, and showed me a handwritten inscription inside the front cover. He read it out loud:

'"Something to keep you on a proper road, love Lilias".

'That's a strange way of saying things, isn't it?' he said.

Thinking You're Not Enough

ANTHEA

The streets were awash with the glow of blue. Street after street, bathed in an unavoidable aquamarine light. It was a fairly new phenomenon in the UK: sunbeds in people's bedrooms and spare rooms. They used to live exclusively in beauty salons, but now people could rent them out, and use them as much as they wanted; whenever they wanted, in their own homes.

Anthea was 14 years old when she first started using them. She was doing an apprenticeship in a hairdresser's and there was a bed onsite. The manager said, 'It's great, you'll love it.' And she did. Then her mum started hiring them; turning the family's pale, white skin to a year-round holiday brown. Another blue light glowing in the darkness.

'If I'm totally honest,' she said, 'I think the addiction started then.'

It was the 1980s and there was a lot we didn't know yet. Things we thought were healthy and good turned out to be anything but. It was also the decade when America made itself comfortable in the living rooms of Britain – with the shoulder pads and perma-tans of *L.A. Law* and *Miami Vice* – when the promise of glamour reached as far as Anthea's town in the north of England.

'I remember the majority of girls at school using them,' she noted. 'They were the latest craze back then, like spiral perms. It was just normal.'

I asked, how many times she would use them?

'Probably two, maybe three times a week,' she replied. 'All from the ages of 14 to 25.

'It's a big chunk, isn't it, really?'

So, every week, for over a decade, Anthea would alternate between using a bed at home and a bed in a tanning salon, laying between a sandwich of light-filled tubes for up to 30 minutes at a time. Burning her skin until it turned a sun-kissed brown.

She liked how it made her feel: healthy, glowing.

'I'd say it was just the addiction of feeling better,' she said. 'That your skin felt clearer and you needed to wear less make-up. If I was going on a night out or there was a birthday coming up or a holiday, I'd go on the sunbed.'

But when the tan faded, the confidence it gave her faded too.

'It's hard to put into words, but that feeling, it was almost like you were losing part of your … it would be like something was missing.

'The desire for a tan, it was just constant.'

Gradually, as she got older, Anthea's life moved away from using the beds. She went from working in beauty to a career in mental health, supporting the victims of abuse. She fell in love, got married. Had two sons. And then one day, she noticed something wasn't quite right.

'There was a little pink pearl-sized lump on my ear,' she said. 'I can remember talking to my hairdresser about it and the hairdresser said, "Just get it checked if it's itching. It doesn't look right."' So, she went to see her doctor. But the doctor took a look and just said it was a wart. Anthea didn't question what they said, she just felt embarrassed; somehow connecting warts with 'being dirty'. She asked the doctor if she should try an over-the-counter remedy and the doctor said she could. But when Anthea did try it, it did nothing. And by the next time she went for a cut and colour, that 'little pink pearl' had grown.

'My hairdresser kept saying that she could see that it was changing slightly. And I said, "Well, it's itchy." If I'm honest, it felt like a reaction to something.'

Over the next few years, Anthea kept going back to her doctor but no other treatment was offered. She would wake in the morning to a white pillow streaked with blood, but still no other treatment was offered. Finally, a concerned nurse passed her case back to the doctor, who referred her to a dermatologist, who referred her to a plastic surgeon, who sent her for a biopsy.

It took Anthea five years for that biopsy to be taken and 10 days for the results to return.

'That appointment was quite an out-of-body experience,' she confessed. 'It was a Friday. I drove because I wanted to keep my mind busy. I'm a big fan of the band James and I had their new album on and it was playing, blasting in the car.'

She picked up her husband, Stephen, or Ste as she calls him, and together they drove to the hospital. But when they pulled into the car park, he went to get out and she kept hold of his hand, not wanting them to move: 'I said, "If we stay here in the car park, if we stay here and don't go in, we stay in the grey area." And he looked horrified. He looked at me scared. As if I was going to say, "I'm not going in."' But in they went, together.

She remembers Wimbledon was playing on the waiting room TV.

She remembers that when the doctor called her name, both she and her husband rose to their feet and she suddenly, out of nowhere, decided she would go in by herself.

'I just went, "It's okay, Ste. Sit down, I've got this." And he looked at me and he went, "What do you mean?" And I just said, "I've got this." And in my heart of hearts, I was trying to protect him from going into that room and hearing what I knew was – what I sensed was coming.'

So Anthea went in alone and the doctor delivered the news she sensed would come: he told her that she had melanoma, that she would need her whole ear amputated and that they would need to do some more scans to see if the cancer had spread to her brain.

Anthea was diagnosed with Stage 3c melanoma: the cancer had already spread to the surrounding tissue and was one step away from spreading to her organs and becoming incurable. She was 39 years old.

Ste joined her in the consultation room as the doctor went off to request the scans. They were alone for a couple of minutes, so Anthea told him what the doctor had told her.

'I always say, in a relationship, it's almost like a seesaw. When one of you is strong, one can be weak. I don't feel like you are ever weak together. And that day, I was strong and my husband was falling apart. It was really hard. And it wasn't that I was feeling strong. I just think it felt reassuring to finally know and think, right, we can deal with whatever this is now. We can deal with it.'

They drove home and broke the news to their sons, who were 13 and 14 at the time.

She confessed that that first night of knowing was hard. 'I stayed up really late,' she remembered, 'because I just needed— I couldn't process any of it. I just played lots of loud music. Because music's a big thing in my life, it's a massive, massive thing. I'm not a big drinker, but I can remember drinking sangria, because it was in the house. I think I got slightly inebriated and was listening to music, just trying to block it out of my mind.'

Even leaving the hospital, waiting to pay for the parking, Anthea says it felt very strange and very surreal. Like someone had pressed mute.

Over the next five years she would go on to have an ear amputated, her inner and middle ear removed, along with all of her salivary glands, a chunk of her skull and her temporal bone. The doctors cut away all that they could to try and create a margin between her body and the cancer, but melanoma is a hard one to detect. Anthea told me to think of a dandelion flower: 'You know a dandelion when it's gone to seed? As a little child if you play What's the Time, Mr Wolf? And you blow it and sometimes the wind was blowing the wrong way and it would blow back into your mouth? Melanoma is supposed to be akin to that. Basically, you can remove it from the site, but the cells can spread anywhere around your body. It can be on the soles of your feet, your toenails, your fingernails, in your breasts, liver, lungs, kidneys, brain. If mine reoccurs now, it will probably not show on my skin, it will show in one of my major organs.'

Anthea admits to feeling an ongoing guilt for having ever used a sunbed and 'causing all of this'. But then her husband, her 'rock', would remind her that she didn't know the dangers back then. No one did. But guilt is such a strange emotion, it doesn't always make logical sense. It made me wonder how the other people involved in Anthea's life felt, knowing about her prognosis?

Her mum brought sunbeds into the family home, week after week; she allowed her kids to use them as much as they wanted. I wondered how she reacted to Anthea's news of having cancer. Had she felt any guilt about that decision?

The fact is, we'll never know. Because when I shared my question with Anthea, she fell silent for a beat, then forewarned me that this was 'where it might get a little bit awkward'.

She told me her mum didn't know about her diagnosis.

That there was a reason why Anthea changed careers from beauty to abuse support: she was a survivor herself. She carefully explained how, after her parents got divorced, her mum remarried and then moved them across the country to start again. That that was when her stepdad started sexually abusing her, from the age of eight.

Nobody knew, or if they did, no one did anything about it. Until years later, when Anthea gave birth to her and Ste's eldest son and she couldn't keep quiet anymore.

She said: 'I spoke out about the abuse because here I am as a mum, a new mum, feeling intensely protective. I mean, I felt that whilst pregnant, that I would kill to protect my child and die protecting them. So fast forward to having just given birth to him and holding him in my arms. I just got this overwhelming urge to speak out, even though my stepdad, as far as I'm aware, only abused me and didn't abuse boys. I just felt that if I didn't speak out, I'm not protecting anyone else.'

So, Anthea told her mum what he had done and then went to the police. Her stepdad was arrested, taken to court and then sent to prison. Initially, her mum supported her but once he was convicted, it became obvious that her mum and stepdad continued to have a relationship, even though she knew what he had done to her daughter. Even though it had been proven in a court of law. And when Anthea made it clear she wasn't happy, her mum gave her an ultimatum: to accept them as a couple, or to lose her forever.

By this time, Anthea's real dad had already died, so her mum was all she had left. She tried to maintain contact for a while, but it ended abruptly when Anthea decided to make a rare visit to see her mum at work and a co-worker started asking her about how her life was.

'She said, "Oh, it's so good to see you. How's Australia?"

'And I looked at her, perplexed. "I don't really know what you mean."

'And she said, "You've emigrated. Are you home? Have you brought the boys?"

"'I've never been to Australia," I said, "I don't really know what you're talking about.""

And then Anthea connected the dots: from the north of England to the other side of the world and back again: 'Rather than tell her friends that her husband was a paedophile and had been sent to prison for sexually abusing her daughter, my mum chose to say that he'd been hospitalised because he was unwell and that I had emigrated to Australia.'

Anthea 'politely' put the co-worker straight and then her mum appeared – 'I just said, "I'd like to know how you sleep at night, Mum. Because no matter who we are, no matter what lies we say to ourselves, we all have a conscience, no matter how deeply buried it is."'

Three weeks later, Anthea received a letter and an answer of sorts.

'It just said, "I'm sorry for being a shit mum. I am a shit mother." But then it went into "You ask me how I sleep at night. I've been diagnosed with fibromyalgia and rheumatoid arthritis. The consultant said it's from the stress of you speaking out. You asked me how I sleep at night. I take the following medications …" She gave me a list. And it was kind of like, no, this isn't what we're doing, Mum. I was asking you how your conscience eats away at you.'

That was 21 years ago and it was the only acknowledgement Anthea would ever really get. She never saw her mum again. Her mum now has dementia, her stepdad is dead. She hasn't spoken to her older brother since the court case because he gave their stepdad a glowing character statement. She lost her younger brother for a while too, due to the family division, but he came back to her.

Although every part of this situation was painful, she's still glad she spoke out.

'I felt immense freedom. Suddenly I felt like his hands were no longer over my mouth. I had spoken out, the police had believed me, my friends, my family that had stayed with me all believed me, and suddenly I felt that what I'd carried all of my life, from the age of eight, was just … I was free of it all.

'At the time of the abuse, he kept telling me that nobody would ever believe me. That if I told anybody, my mum would never believe it and I would lose contact with her. And ironically, the latter happened anyway. But my mum is one of those women that can't be without a male. So much so, that she forgoes her relationship with me. So going back to your question about my mum and telling her about having cancer, that was probably the hardest thing, because I desperately wanted … I'm going to get upset now – I desperately wanted my mum to wrap her arms around me and tell me it was going to be alright.'

Anthea laughs at the improbability of that wish coming true, but then adds, 'So probably the one and only time that I really, really needed her, she wasn't there. To be disowned by the one person in the world that we love, the person we allegedly are supposed to be loved unconditionally by … I have to remind myself that it's not my fault.'

Her body is now mapped by her quest to stay alive. Her bones are now really fragile and can break and crumble at any point; she has a flat piece of skin where her ear once lived, and has tinnitus in the one that remains, which she says screams at her 24 hours a day. 'The only time I don't hear it is when I'm asleep. But it's the last thing I hear at night and it's the first thing I hear in the morning. It's like there's a young girl screaming on my shoulder all the time.'

Radiotherapy has given her cataracts on her left eye, so if she's looking at a screen, her vision can jump around. But, because her ear was amputated, dealing with that can be tricky.

'I sometimes have to wear glasses and obviously without my prosthetic ear I look like a drunk librarian. They don't stay up on the left side,' she laughed. 'No disrespect to any librarians out there, I'm not saying they're all drunk.'

She then recounted a moment when they were on a family holiday and the glue keeping her prosthetic ear in place was tested to its limits: 'You can wear it for about 12 hours before the glue starts to wear off and we were out one day having lunch and my husband just looked, with sheer horror, and I went, "What's wrong?"'

The heat had made Anthea's skin sweat and her prosthetic ear was just about holding on. She laughed. 'Can you imagine that, landing on somebody's table?'

Somehow Anthea manages to keep looking at the strong, sunny side of things. She says cancer has changed her life, but it's also brought some unexpected positives.

'I used to be a very anxious person prior to being diagnosed. I was anxious about turning 40. Because, as with a lot of the things from my childhood, I always told myself that I'm not good enough. But cancer has improved all of that in a strange way. The shit I used to worry about, I don't worry about now. It's kind of like I am good enough and if somebody doesn't like who I am, I can't change that. If somebody doesn't like me, I've come to realise that I've got no control over that. That that isn't my fault.

'What I do now is I focus on every day and live each day,' she said. 'I don't worry about yesterday because I can't change that. I can't change my childhood, I can't change using sunbeds. But what I can change is today.

'I can't worry too much about a year from now,' she added, 'ten years from now, because worrying just spoils today, which, like I say is something cancer brought. So that's a positive I'm truly grateful for.'

Her thoughts about getting old have also changed. She can now see the fallacy of it all.

'I was 39 when I was diagnosed. I was a month off being 40,' she stated. 'I'm not a particularly vain person but from 35 onwards, I was a bit anxious. In my head it was kind of like, am I at the stage in life that I should be at 40? Have I paid enough of my mortgage? Silly things. And then being diagnosed just put all the fear away and flipped it on its head, and just made me think, I'm lucky to be here, do you know what I mean?

'I'll be 45 next month and it's kind of like I wasn't expected to live to this point, so it's now a celebration. Whereas I'd say at 39 it was, "Oh my God, I'm going to be 40. Am I doing all the right things?" It's just strange how things can just turn on a sixpence.'

Every day in the UK, seven people die of malignant melanoma. In the US that number is closer to 25. Sunbeds aren't the only risk factor but it increases your likelihood many-fold, especially if you are young.

'It's ironic that there are people in India buying bleach to bleach their skin lighter, yet here in the UK, people are burning themselves on sunbeds. People are not confident or happy in their own skin. You say to yourself, I can't wear that dress because I've got rolls of fat or whatever. But we've all got them, even the slimmest of people have rolls, haven't they? And even the slimmest people are still not happy, they just want to be slimmer.

'It's almost like we're perpetually told we are not good enough,' Anthea said.

'Some people will go, "Well, if my hair was longer, if my nails were longer …" It's like we just get swept away on this pathway of marketing and fakeness. It's fake boobs, it's nail extensions, it's hair extensions and bum fillers.

'You're aspiring to be a fake version of a fake version. It's just crazy.

'A lot of people aren't content with who they are. If you lined up a hundred women, every single person's body would be different, but we all have our own insecurities.'

And then Anthea talked about where her own insecurities had started: her mum.

'She was generally always overweight and was never happy with her figure. She was always either on Weight Watchers or Slimming World. I grew up with her always telling herself she wasn't good enough and I thought that was normal. I thought that was totally normal. And it's kind of like we're all telling ourselves what we haven't got, instead of engaging with what we have and the beauty we hold.

'That we're always going to be better.

'And by wanting to be better, we're telling ourselves we're not good enough now.'

Anthea laughed at the nonsensical nature of it all.

When she started using sunbeds, she had no idea of the dangers. She had no idea that it would leave her with a life-limiting cancer, with minimal hearing, with constant tinnitus. That her ear would be amputated and she would face the prospect of saying goodbye to all she loves 30 years too soon. She now regrets ever using them. She regrets that she wasn't happy with the way she was born. She regrets that she felt like she wasn't enough.

But everything is different now. Her focus, and everything else.

'I've no idea how long I've got to live,' she said. 'I've got to be careful with how I manage my time. But that's become my new normal, whatever normal is.

'To age is a privilege. It means you're surviving, doesn't it?'

About six months after we spoke the doctors informed Anthea that her skin cancer had spread to her lungs, her bowels, her spine and her brain. She faces yet more tests and

153

treatments, but is buoyed by the enduring love and support of her chosen family, by her husband and her two sons, as she tries to eke out as much extra time as she can get. Music blasting in the background, James once again playing on repeat.

'Find what really matters … ' they sing. 'Right now, right now, right now.'

Missing the Opportunity of a Lifetime

ANNIE

The cruise ship was leaving the UK to sail around the Caribbean for six months. A floating city that would island hop around some of the most beautiful places in the world, supported by flanks of workers below deck. Cooks, cleaners, waiting staff – and hairdressers. Hairdressers like Annie. It was the 1960s. A brief moment in English employment history when people could leave one job in the morning and find themselves in another by the afternoon. It was the time to take chances. To try out new things before marriage and babies wedded you to expectation and mortgage repayments.

But, as that boat sailed out of British waters, Annie knew she had made a mistake. Because it left without her. And 50 years on, she still asks herself why.

Annie is 73 now. She lives on a nice street, in a nice house with large bi-fold doors that lead out on to an even larger garden. Her home is full of books, her kitchen is spotlessly clean and her humour is a touch on the dry side, but many years ago she found herself living a very different life. And it was that life that led her to choose not to be on that boat.

Raised in the south of England she was a post-war baby, born into a small family of understated love and cups of sweet hot tea. Annie became a hairdresser by default. She started doing her mother's hair when she was 12, so when she left school three years later it seemed like an obvious career choice. She began an apprenticeship, met Pam and together they learnt the trade: lining up at the back of the salon, all dressed up in matching pale – mauve roll-necks and tight flared skirts, waiting to be called on to pass hairpins or sweep the floor. In time, Annie and Pam would go from being friends to godparents to each other's children, but until then, they graduated from their course and found jobs at the same hairdresser's.

Then, one day, Pam heard that a cruise ship was recruiting staff. It was the opportunity of a lifetime: months of travelling and meeting new people, a way for a blue-collared girl to earn a living and sample a slice of the world.

Pam told Annie that she had applied and suggested that she apply too. At first Annie said yes, but then she thought, *No, I'll lose him.*

The 'him' she was talking about was Michael. She hadn't known him for long, but they had already become very serious. He was different in all the ways that can turn us from who we really are. Because Michael wasn't a 9-to-5 man. He wasn't an office suit. He was an artist from London who was in her hometown temporarily to make some extra money.

He loved art and jazz and late nights. And she loved him.

'It's funny when you meet somebody that is so outside of your comfort zone. I'd never met anybody who painted pictures before. It was fascinating. I used to feel really proud that he had a studio and that he was an artist, and he was different to everybody else. Do you know what I mean?'

We talked about their early days, before marriage and kids, and the inevitable divorce that would occur further down the track. She had shown me a picture of them together, one of only a handful she'd kept. On the left stands Annie, tall, slim, in a long black dress, her hair piled neatly on top of her head. On the right is Michael. Dapper, smiling. Cheeky. But, she explained, that night of dressing up was the exception rather than the rule.

'I can't remember us ever going anywhere,' she said. 'The only place I ever went was his house. I can't remember ever going out anywhere because he was always wanting to paint. I just used to go round and sit in his garage in the freezing cold and watch him.'

'It's stupid, I can't believe I was so stupid!'

So, Pam sailed away. And Annie stayed behind.

'When you think about it, if he felt that much for me, surely six months wouldn't have made an iota of difference. It was only about six months, it was only for a season.'

'It's something I really regret,' she admitted. 'I felt that I didn't have enough oomph to do what I would have liked to have done, which is quite sad really, when you think, there's only this one bit of life. But I didn't have the wherewithal to do that. And I suppose I feel quite ashamed. I feel ashamed because now I think, what a hypocrite I was when I used to say to my kids, "There's a big wide world out there, go and see it." But I didn't want them to feel the same way I did.

'And so, it has always been a regret, always.

'I can't say I regret marrying Michael,' she added. 'I mean, what would have happened if I hadn't met him? Where would I be? What would I have done?'

She thinks she still would have had children, but, 'I'm sure they wouldn't have been like they are, because they're all part of him. It's two people merged into one, isn't it? With bits from one family and bits from the other.

'I'm a mixture of my mum and dad, and they weren't adventurous. They were just normal, on-the-level people. They wanted good for me, but back then, you weren't encouraged to have a career. You just had a job, women especially.'

Annie explained how 'back then' women couldn't hold bank accounts in their own name; how they were expected to stay at home until they got married and then leave work when they did. How both men and women went straight from their family home to the marital nest with no space in between to explore who they really were and what they really wanted.

'It was a different time,' she said. 'It was a different country.

'To normal working-class people, you just worked and then you had a good time and then you worked and then you had a good time. It was that simple.'

Their marriage would prove to be predictably fraught. All the things that drew Annie to Michael in those early days of courtship, all the ways he was different, were the very things that would destroy them in the end. And after 18 years of her doing all the school runs, all the cooking, all the cleaning, all the worrying about money, while he ended up in other countries, and other beds, she ran out of love: it was time to call time.

'I used to say to myself, when I get sorted I'll do that. And I suddenly realised, you are never sorted. You are never, ever sorted because life throws stuff at you that unsorts you. But that is the way life should be, isn't it? Otherwise you'd go mad, if it was just one long straight road that you could see into the distance.'

Annie was raised when ration books were still in use; when you did what your parents did before you and your prospects were limited. It's no wonder her path led her to Michael and away from the possibilities of working overseas. In her world, picking someone like him, falling in love with someone like him, was already an act of rebellion.

I asked Annie about that cruise and at what point did she realise she'd made a mistake?

'When Pam came back,' she said, 'and showed me the photos. We chatted about it and I thought, I could have done that. *I* could have done that.

'I might have gone, so enjoyed it that I would have spent the rest of my life travelling and gone from ship to ship, which is what some people do. I mean, Pam didn't, but at least she went and tried. I could have absolutely hated it. It could have been six months from hell. But until you do something, you just don't know, do you?

'I wished I'd done it, but I didn't, which is down to me, isn't it? It's just the way I was.

'Looking back, I do feel that I let myself down. But then, I don't suppose anybody goes through life without any regrets, surely?'

Annie's children are grown, her grandchildren are growing. Her parents are gone. Pam is gone, too. And she is left, happy and content: she found love again, with a steady, reliable man who, to her relief, doesn't have a creative bone in his body. Together, they have built a life that has enabled her to travel. To France, to Italy, to America. But never to the Caribbean. She now has the means to go on that cruise, above deck this time, but never has.

Five decades on, Annie confesses to being a homebody, happy to potter around her house and garden, and go overseas once in a while when persuaded. Those shared genes, passed down to her from her 'on-the-level' parents showing themselves once again.

'I do remind myself of my mum,' she confessed. 'Because my dad always wanted to go to lots of places but she always refused.' Her parents spent years saving up to go to New Zealand for their one big adventure together. But just as they'd nearly squirrelled away enough money, her dad's arthritis got worse and he was unable to travel.

New Zealand was their Paradise Falls, but their quest would remain forever undone. Just like Annie's cruise would remain undone, one generation later.

'It just goes to show, you shouldn't put things off, doesn't it? Don't put it off, if it's something you really want to do.

'If opportunities come up, grab them with both hands and go where it takes you.'

Staying in an Unhappy Relationship

KATHY

Romance was everywhere that summer. Diana had just become a princess and love wasn't only in the air, it was on every TV screen in the world. The prospect of finding 'The One' felt obvious then, inevitable even. It was 1981 and two months after the world had watched Charles and Di tie the knot, it was Kathy's turn. She would stand in a little sunny church in the middle of Canada and say 'I do' in front of 50 family and friends, her three-year-old son as ring-bearer.

Kathy is tall, and slim, with a bob of salt and pepper hair. She describes herself as a naive person, someone raised in a deeply religious family who trusts what people tell her. She is also a helper: a mother, a teacher for most of her life, and a volunteer now that the door to work has been closed by age.

We spoke on the phone, her voice thoughtful and patient. She repeated my name throughout our talk, connecting us across continents. I got the feeling that the children she taught were a very lucky bunch. I imagined them sitting in front of her, legs crossed, eager and ready.

I had found Kathy on an online forum about divorce after 60. Her post was very clear, with one particular phrase I couldn't quite forget: 'My only regret is I did not get out sooner.'

In the West, over 50 per cent of marriages end in divorce but few last as long as Kathy's. It was her second, so it was low-key; a wedding dress replaced with a pant suit. She can't remember what music they chose for their first dance, she just remembers how much she wanted to share her life with someone, to be in a partnership and be part of something good.

They honeymooned in Florida for a week and on their return started to put down roots. Between her job in education and his as a contract electrician they managed to afford a big, beautiful house in a quiet neighbourhood. It had more bedrooms than they needed and a huge garden with an inground swimming pool. It was a special place.

Two years later, they welcomed another child into the world – a daughter this time – and their family of four was complete.

As a couple, they went bowling, they golfed, they joined a mixed curling team. They held dinner parties and travelled across Europe, the US, and Canada, all on motorbikes. She surprised him with cooking classes, theatre nights and dinners. They saw *Romeo and Juliet*.

As a family they would rent canoes and paddle through the city. Every Christmas and Thanksgiving they were joined by Kathy's mum for family game time and every Halloween she would make her kids homemade costumes and trick-or-treat around their neighbourhood.

Over the years the garden grew, as the family did, the lawn awash with lilies and poppies. On the surface everything looked perfect, a good life by any measure. But, as with most things, it was more complicated than that. Because it didn't take long before things started to drift and, gradually, what had worked didn't anymore.

He started to work away from home. He never wanted to talk. They ate dinner separately and watched TV apart. 'Like flatmates,' she said. And after years spent snoring beside her, he ended up sleeping in one of the unused bedrooms they had reserved for guests.

When Kathy's daughter graduated from Grade 8, he went golfing.

When there were school concerts, he didn't attend.

They lived separate lives in different parts of the house. And that's how it continued, with Kathy hoping things would change if she just tried a little bit harder.

But things didn't change or get better, the separation simply widened.

'It was like I was there by myself,' she explained. 'I really had set up my own private life. I felt that I was not cared about, the children were not cared about, so I just carried on with our lives and we all lived in the same house.'

Kathy realised she was stuck in a partnership that only worked one way. All the good things they'd done were down to her: the holidays organised, the dinners cooked, the travelling. They weren't what they had created, but what she'd worked towards. She had surprised him with cooking classes and theatre nights, but he had never surprised her.

Not with good things, at least.

But still she stayed, her hope carrying her through her 30s, and 40s, and 50s, and 60s ... She stayed through all the possibilities of something else happening.

I asked her about the beginning and when she knew they would get married.

'I think I conjured up some image in my mind that this was true love and it was going to be great,' she said. 'But it would have been more of a practical idea when I think back.'

Kathy admitted that her decision to marry this 'steady' man had been influenced by the circumstances she found herself in 10 years before, in 1971, when she first said 'I do'.

Husband 1 was a man of the cloth, training to join a Christian ministry. They met at university and he seemed like a 'good' person, someone her family would approve of, given their own religious leanings. They courted for a while, then decided to tie the knot. She put her teaching career on hold and supported him through his studies, the birth of their son and their first five years of marriage. She was busy being a stay-at-home parent, while he was busy going back and forth between the various churches he was training in. It wasn't the partnership she longed for, but it was all she knew.

Until one day, when the truth made itself known: when Husband 1 graduated and his real intentions became clear. He informed Kathy that she had 'served her purpose'. That she had helped present him as a family man and now that he didn't need that façade anymore, she was surplus to requirements. He stopped pretending to try; he ignored her, he acted like she wasn't there and started to make her life intentionally uncomfortable. When Kathy had their son, he didn't attend his birth. In fact, she told me he never even touched him.

He would joke about cutting the brake wires in her car.

He would joke about killing her and becoming free to do as he pleased.

Then the couple attended counselling, and the unravelling continued.

Kathy thought it was just something the ministry expected, to make sure the men they were ordaining – and they were all men in those days – wouldn't bring the Church into disrepute. She soon found out the real reason why.

'He had to take an extra year in a chaplaincy programme and we had to go to marriage counselling. I was told that this was all just part of his course.

'Eventually, I did see what was going on.'

That moment came courtesy of their counsellor, who broke protocol and insisted they talk – 'She knew what was going on,' Kathy said, 'and she knew that I didn't.' The counsellor explained that their sessions weren't part of the usual course; that Husband 1 had been involved with multiple women across the parishes he attended – including having an affair with one married woman and the exploitation of an under-age girl. Counselling was the Church's attempt at rehabilitation. Then she told Kathy that Husband 1 had confessed his intention to get Kathy out of the way so he could do whatever he wanted, unencumbered by his wife and son.

REGRETS OF THE DYING

His threats were real and they were what triggered the coun-sellor to break their confidence and warn Kathy to get out.

'She looked at me and she said, "I'm telling you right now, you need to make arrangements to leave this marriage, take that little boy and never look back."'

So that's what Kathy did. Four years later, enter Husband 2.

The two men were very different. Where Husband 1 was fraudulent and calculating, Husband 2 seemed safe and reli-able. Where Husband 1 had never even held his own son, Husband 2 said he wanted to help raise the boy as his own. So, after three months of dating, they decided to make their union official. There were no grand gestures of romance or love, no going down on bended knee or glasses of champagne to celebrate. This would be a second marriage for both of them, but they seemed like a good fit.

'I didn't really know him that well,' she explained, 'but he had a good job, we had things in common. You think, this could be a good thing.

'I was pretty scared after the end of the first marriage and this felt safe.'

Kathy's first marriage had brought lies, manipulation and the threat of physical violence, so it was understandable that she sought out someone stable. A person who wouldn't let her down.

In the end, it wasn't one specific thing that broke her rela-tionship with Husband 2, more a series of three that finally showed Kathy it was time to move on.

The first was when she was diagnosed with breast cancer. Her treatment was intensive. She had to go to hospital for drug therapy, but he wasn't interested in going with her so she drove herself, every three weeks for over a year. He didn't even want her to mention it.

'I was told to be quiet, that he didn't want to hear about it.'

And still she stayed, hoping things would change.

Then, halfway through her treatment, Kathy realised that large sums of money had been going missing from their joint bank account. She called Husband 2, worried that they'd been scammed, wanting to freeze their accounts and plug the financial leak – until he admitted that he was the one who had taken the money and gambled it away. That he'd dipped into their financial safety net whenever he felt the need to go to the casino. Into her pension, into their savings. Kathy felt gut-punched, sick, but she knew she had to focus on staying alive: 'My goal shifted to deal with the cancer,' she said, 'and I didn't say any more about it, I just watched the bank accounts.'

The gambling continued, the money trickled out and they ended up in counselling. On the first session the therapist suggested her husband needed to get specific help with his addiction, but he refused, then stopped attending. And that was that: no more counselling.

And still she stayed, for another two years. The hope of something better carrying her along, just. Talking to her reminded me of my own situation: clinging onto an unhappy relationship in the hope that things would get better. Trying not to hurt other people and hurting myself in the process.

It's hard to know when to let go. To know when enough is enough. For Kathy, the third and final straw came quietly. He didn't have an affair, or become violent. He did what he always did: he put himself first.

His birthday was in the April and Kathy's was a couple of months later, in July. He secretly bought himself an expensive motorbike, a BMW, without checking if they could afford it first and once again put them into debt. Then Kathy's birthday arrived, 60 days later. She had organised her own dinner with friends, all he had to do was show up.

'I was getting dressed and he says, "Where are you going?" He had completely forgotten.'

So, she went on her own. That was the end: she had finally had enough.

And within the month, at the age of 70, an age when most couples are settling into their retirement, she left. She packed her things and moved out of the house she loved, the place she had raised her children. It was over, she was free.

They had been together for 36 years.

There were no blazing rows. No slamming of doors or smashing of plates. No pleading to do better or try more. She left their house the way she had lived there: like a lodger in her own life, invisible to a man who would never truly realise what he had lost.

By the time Kathy left, her children were grown with families of their own and they supported her decision. Her grandkids said they missed the house, with its books and games, now boxed up and given away; the swing in the garden left to sway in the breeze without them. Kathy explained that there was no love there anymore and that there would be other fun places. But she understood how they felt. She missed her garden too, so volunteered to help friends and community groups with theirs to fill the gap. She missed her beautiful home, so after a couple of years of moving around, she bought a plot of land in her old neighbourhood and has just started to build a new home there. It will be different this time, it will be all hers.

'Deep down, I wanted to be in a partnership,' she said. 'And I guess I realised this wasn't a partnership of any kind. If you give somebody a chance and they say, "I'll make a change and this will be different," and they do, that's one thing. But when you realise over and over again that it's not, then you've got to say to yourself, you deserve more than that.'

I asked Kathy 'what if…?' What if she hadn't held on for 36 years? What if she had left him sooner, what would her life be like now?

She paused for a second, 'Well, that's the thing I regret …' she said.

Her voice started to falter. She fell silent. 'I don't want to look back, I don't want to think back, you know? I can't go back and undo things but I am upset I didn't stand up for myself.

'Why did I not expect better? Why did I keep hanging onto that?

'Maybe I was afraid that the marriage would end and then I'd be on my own.

'You hope that it will change,' she admitted. 'But if it doesn't, in a way it takes away from everything else that you love in your life too, because it's constantly on your mind. You just feel neglected. People always say that about abuse, but neglect is a form of abuse as well. I know for my children, that's what they experienced.

'I always felt that I was out there by myself. It's a lonely feeling. And it doesn't have to be that way.

'What could I have done to make a difference?' she wondered. 'I couldn't have done anything, because it's a two-way street, right? If that relationship was in any way meaningful to him, he should have been part of it and he never was.

'Why waste time?' she added. 'Because then you're depriving yourself of meeting somebody that you could love a lot better, and might love you, or would love you. I need to figure out why I didn't feel I deserved more. And I think that's the part I have to forgive myself.'

Kathy doesn't think she'll find love now, she thinks it's too late. But she still believes in it, and in relationships: 'I see it all around me,' she said. 'I see people that really care about each other and are there for each other.

'What is love?' she questioned. 'For me, now, it is a feeling that somebody cares about me, that they've got my back and will be there for me. And between the two marriages, and 43 years, I've never felt that. If you are in a relationship where the other person doesn't really involve you or take any interest in what you're doing, or if you have a significant situation in your life and they're not there, pack it in. Pack it in, because you deserve a lot better.

'Life is just too short to let someone steal it away.

'I am far better off on my own,' she admitted. 'It was hard at first because if I'd still been in the working world, it would have been a lot easier to meet people, but that's the great thing now about the internet. You can go online and meet a whole new group of friends.

'Somebody once said: "I know what I can bring to the table, which is why I'm not scared to eat alone." In the end, I walked away with the most loving person in that relationship: me. And all the things I gave up, I actually found a way to replace them.

'I have a lot to be thankful for.'

Kathy is now cancer-free. She now goes to concerts, and galleries, and meets new people. She has plans to travel and enjoy the world. She has always done these things, she never stopped. But, because her ex-husband didn't want to do them too, she felt guilty leaving him at home alone. She doesn't feel like that anymore, the guilt has been replaced with better things.

The landscape of Kathy's life has changed forever. She's ended up alone in spite of it all, but less alone than she was. She was trapped by the hope that things would get better and is now free to make that happen for herself. Now her quiet moments are filled with friends and family and art and travel. She lost the garden she loved, so she created another. She moved away from the house she called home, so she's building a new one.

She's building everything anew.

Part Four

HARD
DECISIONS

'You write your life story by the choices you make.
You never know if they have been a mistake.
Those moments of decision are so difficult.'

— *Helen Mirren* —

Not Following Your Gut Instinct

ANONYMOUS

The email address was no more than a series of letters and numbers, too random to be permanent; a burner account that didn't seem to want, or expect, a reply. I had circulated notices around some of my local libraries and day centres, politely enquiring if anyone would like to talk, but in the first few weeks had received zero response. Until one morning, when 'Anonymous' appeared in my inbox.

Their message was only a couple of paragraphs long, with no opening greeting or closing goodbye, so I have no idea who they are, or where they live. This is what they wrote:

I regret not seeing how ill my son had become with end-stage Hodgkin's lymphoma. I regret not being able to keep my promise to be with him in his final week – because I had a throat infection, I daren't go near him. And then he died, suddenly.

I knew that he was terminally ill. No treatment would save him. Yet he was so determined to face chemo I didn't want to pass on my infection and delay the start of his treatment. I should have said to hell with the risk. I should have gone to his side. But I obeyed protocol and stayed away.

The next time I saw him he was dead.

I held him in my arms, knowing that he would never speak to me again.

I regret every moment I didn't spend with my son in those last weeks.

Not Speaking Up

JO

I first met Jo when she was a teenager. Her hair was a mass of tight, dark curls. Her speech very fast, her diction very correct; our conversations peppered with talk of the books she'd read and historical events long past, all delivered with a hands-in-the-air level of enthusiasm.

But that was then. Now she was 32. A fully fledged adult, living in a two-storied flat-share in London, and I was there to talk about a life-changing decision she had made five years ago. Of a moment when she decided to be tested for a type of early onset dementia that runs in her family; a decision that brought into focus the amount of time she had spent not standing up for herself and not speaking out for someone else.

She greeted me with a hug and we settled into her living room. A telly in the corner, a well-worn sofa covered in cushions facing it. We hadn't seen each other for a year or so, but she hadn't changed a bit. She was still amazing company. Still quick, and bright, and funny. She also still had no filter: if

REGRETS OF THE DYING

she feels something, or thinks something, it just comes out. A fully formed thing, neatly tucked in at the edges.

It's strange, talking to people you think you know. It doesn't take long before you realise you know nothing at all. Jo and I had chatted at dozens of gatherings over the years. She'd always seemed improbably young, surrounded by various cousins and offspring, telling jokes and wild stories while I would hide in the kitchen trying to be useful.

If I'm honest, I was jealous. Her side of the extended family had houses with names rather than numbers and educations that stretched way beyond the legally required minimums. They also had a wonderfully carefree eccentricity and a penchant for using names more than once, like they were preparing for Noah's next flight: two Sams, two Jos, two Richards. My own kin were (and still are) very different. A birthday celebration for us wasn't a marquee on the lawn, it was a freshly bought Viennetta with a single candle stuck in the top.

She comes from a family of four: a mum, a dad, herself and her younger brother. She talks about her brother a lot. I had always known about the 'illness', but had never heard anyone discuss it in any great detail, especially not about that moment they first realised there was a problem. For Jo, it happened while she was away, working in her first full-time job after graduating from university.

She had called her mum to arrange a visit home, but was told she couldn't come. That her mum had suddenly lost her job and had to move out of the boarding school where she lived and worked; that her behaviour had become increasingly erratic and she was no longer able to perform her role properly. At first, her employers thought Jo's mum had developed a drinking problem, but a genetic test was carried out and she was diagnosed with a familial type of frontotemporal dementia, or FTD: an uncommon type of dementia that causes problems with behaviour and language.

FTD is like Alzheimer's disease, but different.

Our brains contain billions of nerve cells that send and receive messages. When a person has dementia those nerve cells become damaged and gradually start to die. With Alzheimer's, this death eventually happens across the whole of the brain, which leads to changes in cognition, making people forget things. But with FTD it is the cells that are housed in two very specific areas of the brain – the frontal and temporal lobes – that are affected; the areas of the brain that control our ability to retrieve words, comprehend speech, and regulate our inhibitions.

It's a disease that doesn't make you forget things exactly, not people and places like Alzheimer's disease and vascular dementia can, but how to do things: how to behave, how to talk, how to understand what things mean. It can also lead to people gradually becoming more compulsive, sexually inappropriate, aggressive, rude or even violent. It can make its presence known while you're in your 30s, 40s or 50s. Young, basically. And when it does, you have anywhere between three and 15 years left to live.

The moment her mum tested positive, Jo and her brother realised they had inherited a 50:50 chance of developing it too. Because, like blue eyes or bad teeth, the type of FTD she had was genetic and ran in their family. It had already claimed their great-grandfather, their grandmother and three uncles and aunts, all on their maternal side and all dead by the age of 60, so they knew it wasn't a disease that skipped a generation or discriminated by gender or lifestyle. They knew that no matter what they did or how they lived, the result would be a binary one.

They would either be positive or negative. There was no grey.

Before the development of genetic testing, families who might have been carrying a fault in their DNA would simply hope for the best, or live unaware of the legacy they could be passing on. But now, in most cases, they have a choice: to be tested and find out, or not.

The moment her mum was diagnosed, Jo decided to find out. Her decision was immediate, but the process itself is an understandably lengthy one, with lots of checks and measures along the way. You're required to go to counselling for an hour, every two weeks, sometimes for up to five years. You're asked to articulate why you want to get tested, what you think the result will be, and how you think this will affect you.

You're asked to imagine what it would be like if you were positive. You're asked why you believe it's so important to know, and you're made to explore the idea of regretting that decision to find out, because what is known cannot be unknown.

Inevitably, some won't cope as well as they'd imagined. A positive diagnosis can feel like setting off a ticking clock, counting down the time you have left, drowning out all that is good around you. A negative result can be almost as hard to live with, especially if a sibling has tested positive and you become the 'lucky one' overnight.

Only 20 per cent[6] of people who go through genetic counselling decide to get tested.

That year of contemplation, of chasing an answer, must have felt like a difficult and long road, but Jo was always going to be part of that 1 in 5 minority. She said: 'They found it very hard to persuade me to think of a future in which I would not have FTD. My argument was, if I don't have it, I've got all the time in the world to figure out my future.'

The morning of her test, Jo travelled to central London. She walked into the consultation room, sat down and waited. After months of counselling the answer came swiftly and without ceremony. Jo was told her test result was positive, that she had FTD. Just like her aunts and uncles before her. Just like her grandmother. Just like her mum.

After a brief pause, she double-checked she'd heard them correctly, then she said, 'that was it'. There was no going back. She went to the pub with a group of her closest friends, had lunch and a lot of drinks, then went to London Zoo for the day. It must have been a rather surreal outing: a group of tipsy twenty-somethings, surrounded by tourists, cheering themselves up at the penguin enclosure.

Jo's rapid, almost bullet-point retelling of what happened sometimes makes it seem like she's talking about somebody else. She admits she tends to take bad news well, but also that she was already convinced her result would be positive. That it had been 'a deliberate tactic to believe the worst'. That 'it was much better to believe my result would be positive and then I wouldn't be surprised. I spent a long time crushing hope, basically.'

So much of Jo's world has changed since her diagnosis. She knows her life will be shorter than most. She knows that every decision she makes is now informed by her positive result – dating, relationships, children, work, finances. Thinking you may have a genetic illness is one thing, but having those fears confirmed is another. It's hard to imagine functioning day-to-day without this knowledge seeping into all corners.

I asked how finding out she had FTD had changed her life.

'I became quite desperate to do everything and quite manic and then exhausted,' she told me. 'I became more aware of what progress I'd made, which I guess is a bit like taking account of how I've spent my time.'

She started to care less about enjoying what she was doing and focused more on whether there was even a point to doing it in the first place. She wanted to know if it was going to last and questioned if it was just another thing that would waste time she no longer had to spare.

Time and its passing seemed to redefine everything.

'I find it much harder to relax and enjoy the moment now because I'm always worrying about it being a meaningful experience. It's an attitude I wouldn't have had before. Even if your result is negative, your whole world changes because this thing you've been worried about has been removed,' she told me. She brushed her hair away from her face, then added, 'I think it can be quite difficult to deal with sometimes, particularly because you're not the only person in your family who is at risk.'

Jo's generation holds six more people in direct risk of having FTD, but she wasn't talking about them: she was talking about her brother. He had also been tested, about a month after Jo, but his result came back negative. He is free from all the decisions and dilemmas that his sister will have to face, but not from the effect of them. Jo said that telling him was the hardest part of all. That he probably felt worse about her result than she did, especially once he got the all-clear. Understandably, their relationship has changed. She says that she has always 'felt responsible for him because he had depression since he was probably about 14, quite severe depression. I am much more robust than he is; he's always been much more vulnerable emotionally than me, and he's my little brother.' So, she looked out for him, and after him, because 'there was no one else to do it.'

She says their relationship has become more balanced now that she has her own problems and her capacity has narrowed; that she's less like a mum, and more like a sister.

I asked Jo, knowing all that she knows, knowing all the decisions it has forced her to make and how her life and relationships have changed, does she regret being tested?

Her reply was quick, and clear, and not what I had expected.

'No,' she said. 'Definitely not. I think I'd feel exactly the same, because I just would have been worried. I feel I'd have to assume I was positive in order to be sensible.'

Would it be better knowing how long you have to live so you can make the most of it, or to live in blissful ignorance, taking things as they come? I thought Jo would have wanted to turn back the clock. To unknow her positive result so she could live without it hanging over her head. But she didn't. She has FTD whether she likes it or not, and she is adamant she made the right decision.

Then I asked if there was anything she did regret.

'I regret things like I didn't master organisational skills,' she said. 'I regret things like I'm a terrible procrastinator and I really, really wish I wasn't, because I know I've wasted time. That's the kind of thing I regret, but then I still do it. So clearly, this regret is of limited impact.

'I regret the things which hold me back from doing better, rather than the things I've done. Once the moment is gone, there's not much you can do about it.

'I wish I'd got all that living dangerously, pushing boundaries stuff out of the way,' she told me. 'Good God, I really wish I'd got drunk when I was like 14, in a church-yard, with a load of other people … I don't know if I really do, but it would have been more fun to have got that out of the way first.

'And maybe if I hadn't been so good all the time and scared of misbehaving. I was always scared of being bad and I think perhaps I should have been a little bit more relaxed about it. But I don't think that I'm responsible for a lot of things that have happened to me so I shouldn't really regret them. It's not my job to do that.

'If I'd had a healthier family dynamic, I'd be in a better position to say how testing positive affected me. To be honest,' she admitted, 'there was a lot of other stuff going on.

'It wasn't the worst thing in the world at that time.'

I knew Jo's parents had taught at the same school then divorced after her dad 'ran off' with another member of staff, but I thought, before the affair, they had been a fairly strong and stable family.

I was wrong.

'We had quite a difficult upbringing in some ways,' she said. 'My dad was ... I think the term is "emotionally abusive". He was very violent in a non-physical way. Very controlling, very inconsistent, and because my mum worked, my dad looked after us a lot. He had quite a lot of issues. Like he would lose his temper over things one day and wouldn't notice them the next. Or he would send us to bed at 6 o'clock one night and then keep us up till midnight the night after.'

Jo said that was quite common, the ever-shifting boundary lines that separated the good from the bad, and the bad from the acceptable. If he had something to tell Jo and her brother, then he wouldn't wait until the morning, he would just wake them up in the middle of the night.

'It would be quite confusing,' she said, 'and quite tense.'

One of the stories she told me was about how her brother was sent off to get his hair cut on a Sunday but all the barbers were shut. Too scared to return without the job being done, he'd stay out for hours but by the time he got home their dad had forgotten why he'd sent him out in the first place and normal life resumed.

'I mean, he adored us and then he would forget it for 20 minutes if we were annoying him and then he would remember again and it was as though nothing had happened. But to us of course, it was like a trauma. And now, when we try and talk to him about it, it's like it never happened. It's quite a weird experience actually, because you feel like you made it up, except my brother and I were both there and we tend to remember.'

She admitted that she, 'Spent a very long time hating my dad, like really intensely hating my father, and I think I realised that it was really pointless because he didn't notice.'

Jo said she felt the need to protect her mum from the truth, that somehow, 'she couldn't have handled it because she adored Dad so much. She'd say things like, "I do find it odd how you always annoy your father." And I was like, "What? It's remarkably easy!"'

'I used to think she was generally vulnerable and now I think she did it on purpose, because it's more obvious now that she is less able to conceal the workings of it. You can see the cogs whirling round when she is working out who she wants to talk to about something because she knows she can get round them. You can predict her behaviour.'

Jo shuffled in her seat, then circled back to the idea of regret.

'I wish my dad had left when I was about four, but I don't know, and it is a bit of an unfair picture of him because he was wonderful a lot of the time.

'I wish perhaps I hadn't spent so much of my childhood worrying about my mother and instead asked why she wasn't doing her job. But I think in reality, I wouldn't have done it any differently, because I think I just did what I felt was right at the time.'

Again, she was talking about her brother – and about his long and deep depression.

'No one gave a damn for 10 years,' Jo told me. 'I used to tell them, "He's got depression, you should deal with this. Bye, I'm going back to uni now." But nothing was done. My parents had not dealt with it, and not dealt with it, and it's quite a long way to come back from that. I get quite angry with my mum for her complete failure to look after him when she was capable of it.'

She realises that it's unlikely she'll ever have a heart-to-heart conversation with her parents that will fix everything, but that her main aim in life now is to do better than her mum did. Which, she admits, 'is a bit harsh when Mum is, generally speaking, such a lovely person. But I think being lovely, where does it get you in life if you're not doing anything to help? And she didn't do anything.'

Jo said, 'I think Mum's always just wanted to be looked after and not have to make any hard choices her whole life. She was very young when her mum became ill and I think was basically left alone with her for weeks at a time, because my grandfather never stopped working or reduced his hours.' And then when her grandfather died, her mum, as Jo put it, 'was a wreck. She absolutely worshipped him to the point where she kept his clothes and never threw them away, and had pictures of him everywhere.'

I asked how her parents reacted to the news she had inherited FTD.

'My dad's never mentioned it again and Mum, I think, has rather forgotten it, deliberately in her case.'

All those years of not speaking up for her brother, or herself, has left Jo carrying the load. Her father – the man her mother adored above all else – has moved on, her brother still has depression and her mother is ill. Basically, the buck has stopped at Jo. She's arranged her mum's finances. She's taken out a mortgage so that her mum has a house to live in and has had to become her power of attorney. Effectively, she's had to come to terms with her own diagnosis while looking after a parent who didn't necessarily look after her.

I had to keep reminding myself how young Jo really is.

And this situation, of her mum needing care, is only going to become more pressing, because the FTD is already changing her: she laughs a little too late at jokes, her gait has widened, her walk has slowed, and while she used to relish being part of any raucous debate on offer, she now seems to find it difficult. A distance has developed. A delay between her hearing and seeing things, and reacting to them. Like she's watching life play out in a foreign language, a language that will gradually become more and more impenetrable as the FTD takes hold.

Then she told me about one of her aunts who had also been ill and the day she forgot how to stand up and needed Jo's help to move. She could physically do it, but her mind had completely forgotten how. It made me think of all the things yet to come. About how Jo sees her future and what she wants to achieve with whatever time she has left.

So many people have a plan of where they want to be: the ages they'd like to fall in love and settle down, or buy their first home, or have children, moments time-stamped in their mind years in advance. But Jo told me she'd never had a clear vision of what her life would be like at any particular age. She'd never had any specific goals to be achieved and now tends to see her life more in terms of what she can't have, rather than what she can.

'I could just go on forever with all the things I can't have,' she said. 'Kids are the most obvious. I could never have one on my own. It absolutely could never happen. Who would look after them?' She had considered fostering or adoption, but no longer feels either is feasible, now she knows she won't have a long-term stake.

'I have no choice,' she added, then paused for a moment and gathered her thoughts. I felt this lack of choice must be the hardest consequence to live with, especially as it's a decision she's been forced to make. I remember the longing I felt wanting a child and not being able to have one or stay pregnant. For years, every pram I passed, every toddler I saw reaching for their mother's hand would make my heart churn. Now I have my daughter, it's impossible to imagine life without that little pile of shoes dumped by the front door.

I wondered if Jo thought she would ever find a partner and settle down.

She said, 'I don't think I was so keen on being in a relationship beforehand. I think I always figured I would meet someone in my 40s. I would be one of those late developers because I am quite a late developer and now it's not an option. I really don't think that I ever thought about it until I did genetic testing. That was the first time in my life when I actually thought about what my future was about. I think it's partly because all I ever wanted to do was go to university and leave home.

'I didn't want to be like my parents,' she added.

Jo achieved her dream of leaving home when she left to study history, but in the end, she did follow her parents' path, by going into teaching.

Five years have passed since she tested positive and her life is different because of it.

She decided not to have children once her diagnosis was clear; she has opted to focus on her friends and having fun rather than spending her time building some grand career that would take her away from living. She already thought she had the illness so, in a way, having it confirmed stopped her from worrying about it and helped her to try and focus on all the good things she already had. And her regrets weren't really about not dating or not having enough fun when she was younger, something I thought she might regret now she knows her time is restricted. They were about the things she thought she should have done or could have said. Things that had been orbiting her family for years. But deep down she hadn't done or said those things for good reason – she feared her dad might have withdrawn his love, that her mum wouldn't have listened – and there was no way to turn back the clock now.

'I think I do feel a lot more furious with the universe than I ever was before,' she said, straightening in her seat. 'Because I never used to believe that life was unfair.

'I do sometimes feel cursed, I feel cursed quite often. But then I'm one of these people, it would only take one good thing to happen and immediately I'm the luckiest person ever.'

Jo offered me another cup of tea and we took a quick break. We'd been talking for a couple of hours and it was nearly time for me to leave. Soon the streetlights would illuminate and the roads would fill with rush-hour traffic. I glanced at the notepad resting on my lap, knowing there was one last question I wanted to ask. A tough one: about how Jo viewed death and how she thought her own ending would be. I braced myself, worried that I would upset her in some way. But she wasn't upset.

I asked the question and Jo answered, with pure, logical honesty.

'I've never been particularly afraid of dying in an abstract sense,' she replied. 'Obviously, I might change my mind when it actually happens, but it's always seemed to me a silly thing to worry about, because everyone dies.'

A lot of us shy away from the thought of death. We think that if we speak its name, we'll summon it to our doorstep prematurely. But in Jo's case, it wasn't at her doorstep, it was already inside with its feet up on the coffee table.

Maybe that's why she's so open about it, and so level-headed.

We talked about what was better, going fast or going slow; knowing you're running out of time and being able to prepare, or going quickly without notice.

'I'd much rather know, because I never wanted to die quickly. Ever. I'd much rather die of something and know it was happening and be able to come to terms with it. Perhaps I have a rather weird, wrong idea of what it's like.

'I'd always assumed I would be aware,' she said.

'I think I'd almost enjoy the sensation of knowing I was dying, if I was in my right mind. But obviously, I don't think I will be. It does rather take the fun out of it, because I've always been quite fascinated by the idea of how life stops and where you go afterwards and how you prepare.

'Ultimately, to know that someone is dying and to know that you're saying goodbye to them is probably better than them vanishing from your life unexpectedly. Possibly not the build-up, but the after-effect is probably better that way round.'

And then Jo did what I've seen her do so many times before: she turned away from the darkness of it all and found that one, thin sliver of light.

'I suppose one of the advantages of having an illness like this is there's an astounding chance that all my friends will still be alive, so they can all come to my funeral. Which is probably better than being the last one to go.'

The ritual of a religious goodbye and the idea that she would be surrounded by family and friends seemed to give Jo comfort. As I listened, I imagined what her wake would be like: finger food and cups of steeped tea. A great big display board of photos tacked up in a wonderfully drafty village hall, snapshots of a life cut short. A room full of anecdotes dying to be swapped and shared: about how Jo used to scramble around on the floor at family gatherings, telling jokes and wild stories surrounded by kids that weren't her own.

They will talk about how beautiful and strong she was and how, even at the end, she was thinking of others. Happy to be making them happy even though she knew she wouldn't be there to enjoy it herself.

'I've spent a long time trying to plan the music,' she told me.

'I would have Purcell's *Hear My Prayer, O Lord* because it's the most depressing piece I've ever heard in my life. Everyone would be sobbing, and then I'd follow it up with Paul Simon's, 'Me and Julio Down by the Schoolyard', because it's the happiest piece of music in the world and you can't really be miserable when you're listening to that.'

Keeping a Secret

MILLICENT

On the surface, it seemed like a safe town. A place where you could leave your back door open and your keys in the ignition. A small village in New Zealand where everyone knew everyone else. But what Millicent saw that dark summer's night, and the secret she was then forced to keep, would stay with her forever.

I met Millicent in her self-contained bungalow. She was 94 at the time, but still physically able and fiercely independent. Surrounded by fluffy white throws and china figurines, she explained what life was like back in the 1930s and how different it was to now.

'We lived in the last road in town,' she said. 'We had a big half-acre section with chickens running free and a vegetable patch.'

She told me how quiet it was, and how rural. There was a daily milkman, an egg man, two postal deliveries a day and a fruiterer that would come to your house with a hamper of goods you could choose from. Not that they needed much from the outside world: Millicent's dad kept their vegetable patch well-stocked, growing onions, potatoes, carrots and parsnips.

A river flowed down the back of their property, so when Millicent and her five siblings went swimming, their mum would keep an eye on them from the kitchen and open the window when it was time to come home, calling out 'Teatime! You've been there long enough!'

But it wasn't all picture-perfect. As she entered her teenage years the world was in the grips of the Great Depression, an economic tsunami caused by the 1929 Wall Street Crash. In New Zealand, unemployment rose to an estimated 30 per cent and those who managed to stay in work had their wages slashed, wages that barely covered living costs to begin with.

'People were suffering,' she said. 'A lot of them were having to start all over again. It hit the street like anything, because most of the men lost their jobs and all their savings had gone. Women would commit suicide because they had no money coming in and they had nothing in the house.

'That was quite common down there, not the murders, you know. The suicides.'

Millicent recalled an incident from that time. Not the one that led to her regret, but of something connected: of a boy who went swimming in the river behind their house and never made it home. The police searched for him, they even sent down a diver, but found nothing. About a week later, a child was running through the sand hills to the beach and fell over his body. He'd swallowed a bottle of Jeyes cleaning fluid. He was only 17 – a young boy who saw no future.

In those days children grew up quickly. They were expected to do their fair share around the house, and with few of the magical gadgets we take for granted now, it could be time-consuming and back-breaking work. But for Millicent's mum, it was more than that.

'My mother always used to say, "I want the house cleaned by eight o'clock, I want it clean enough for the Queen." I had two siblings above me and three below, but I got all the work to do. Tuesday was ironing day; Thursdays, the house had to be spring cleaned; Fridays was wash day. The kitchen table had to be scrubbed after every meal and then a cover put on it. She had a lovely big lounge, but I can't remember ever sitting in it – she wouldn't let us go in, we weren't allowed.

'I always did the shopping. I can still remember the prices of things, too. Soap, 4 pence a cake. Dates, 4 pounds of dates for a shilling. Milk was only thruppence a pint.

'Our upbringing was very strict,' she explained. 'Because Mum had six children, she had to make sure that we behaved ourselves. Dad was different. He was easy-going and happy. He was quite content. I never heard him angry, but my mother made sure we didn't stray.

'She was very, very strict,' she repeated. 'We weren't allowed to play with the children on either side of where we lived. That house had three children, this house had six, but we weren't allowed to mix with them. We had to stay in our own backyard and talk over the fence.'

I asked Millicent why. She replied, matter-of-factly: 'Mum said she had enough kids of her own, without any more coming in. Well, she had a point, in a way.'

There was no TV back then either, it hadn't been invented yet, so at night they used to gather together as a family and listen to the radio, or play a record on their prized gramophone. They'd listen to Caruso, Millicent said, 'all the old singers. We thought we were made. We were, really.

'In those days,' she continued, 'the street lights used to go out at about half past 10 as soon as the picture theatres stopped. Young girls did not go out at night alone.'

And then our conversation turned to what happened, eight decades earlier. When Millicent was 15 or 16, and wanting to get a job: 'There was a lady,' she said, 'a Mrs Walker, who lived at the far end of the street. She was a beautiful knitter. And when she saw that I was interested, she said to me, "You come along and I'll teach you how."'

With no job, no money and nothing much to do, Millicent jumped at the chance of a bit of freedom and walked to the far end of the street every afternoon so Mrs Walker could teach her how to knit. And every afternoon she would pass this particular house. It seemed different, somehow. The garden neater; the lady who lived there taller, more elegant.

Millicent said: 'She was just beautiful. I'd put her age at about 35, 36. And she dressed like a chocolate box lady, typically English.' There was a man who lived there too. 'I don't know what he did for a living, but he was always well-dressed, like a commercial traveller could be. He was well-dressed, like she was always well-dressed.

'I never saw her untidy, no matter what time she went out in that garden.'

Millicent watched out for the lady every time she passed. She recalled how she would appear carrying a little pair of gardening gloves and a flower basket, wearing a hat to protect her delicate skin from the harsh New Zealand sun. In an era of patched knees and darned stockings, it's understandable why a teenaged Millicent would become beguiled.

'She was beautifully made up, she was really elegant. And every time I'd look at her, I'd think, I wish I grew up like that, you know, and had a nice house.'

In Millicent's mind that 'nice house' held as many memories as the elegant lady who lived in it. Because all these years on, she could describe it in minute detail. Its big bay windows, the front door, the five steps leading up to it.

And then one day, for one day only, Millicent's routine changed.

'I had a lovely pattern for a lacy jumper. It was only simple but I couldn't work it out, so Mrs Walker said, "I'll show you next time." But she said, "I can't see you tomorrow, come to me in the evening."' So, Millicent did as she was told. She went back the next evening, to learn how to knit that lacy jumper.

'It was summer,' she said. 'A lovely warm, balmy night.' She left home at 6 o'clock. She recalls: 'I just had my knitting with me. And I only had a summer frock on. No cardie. No cardie or anything like that. And shoes. Everybody had cheap sand-shoes in those days 'cause you could run faster in sandshoes.'

And as she always did, Millicent glanced up at that lady's front garden as she passed. It was empty, but she could tell she'd been out there: the plants were newly cut, the hedge neatened.

'Anyway,' she continued, 'I went and got there alright, but I didn't realise how fast the time had gone, you know? Else I wouldn't have seen what I saw.'

She was meant to be home by nine, because it would have still been light then. But somehow, by the time Millicent and Mrs Walker realised how late it was, it was already a quarter past 10: 'So, I grabbed up my knitting and started off down the road.'

She half-walked, half-ran towards home. But this time, as she approached the lady's house, she could hear screams.

'I stopped and I listened. The screams got louder. I could hear her saying. "No! No! No!" And I thought, what's going on here?'

Millicent found a gap in the fence and peeped through.

'The front door was wide open,' she said. 'A passage light on. The lady came running down and as she came down the steps, she had her hands up like this, "No! No! No! No!" and ran towards the flower patch that bordered the drive. She came running down and I could see him coming down the passage after her. He was running too. But she was ahead of him by about six feet and then she turned round, still with her hands up. She turned round – to find him rushing, running out after her. And, she said, "No! No! No!" That's what made me remember, her going "No! No! No!", and he just went biff! He punched her.

'She went backwards, fell backwards about three or four paces. I started to run for my life. I was frightened. I'd seen something I shouldn't, you know?'

And as Millicent ran for her life, the town clock hit 10.30 and all the street lights switched off, throwing her into pitch-black darkness.

'I was terrified,' she said, 'I didn't scream, I didn't want anyone to know I was running. If anyone had of attacked me, if I had screamed, nobody would have heard me.'

The streets were empty: everybody had gone home.

'That's when I ran for my life. I ran and ran and ran. And I could see my mother coming towards me. I'd never been used to hearing matrimonial arguments or fights, I wasn't used to that. I hadn't ever even seen a fight among couples. I'd never seen a man hit a woman. Not like the punch he gave her, anyway. It sent her back three or four paces.'

By the time Millicent reached home it was 20 to 11. She was late, *very* late. And her mum 'set upon' her, annoyed that her usually compliant daughter had broken the rules. So, breathless, shaken, she shared what she had seen and what she had heard: that a woman had been attacked and she was worried for her life.

But her mum didn't go for help – quite the opposite, in fact.

'She said, "You get home to your bed. We'll keep this just between you and me." I had told her every detail and she swore me to secrecy.'

Millicent went to bed and started to doubt what she had seen. Had she imagined it? Did she really see what she thought she had seen? Maybe it was just an argument? Six hours later, she realised that it was very real indeed: 'I got up the next morning. The headline along the bottom of the paper – "Mrs so-and-so found in garden with her throat cut".'

Millicent rushed to show her mother the newspaper article, telling her once again that they should go to the police. But, once again, her mother refused.

'She said, "That's nothing to do with us. I'm not having the police coming to the house." 'And I said, "Well, I'll go down there then."

'And she said, "No, you won't. You'll keep your mouth shut."

'I should have told the police there and then,' she confessed. 'I should have spoken but Mum didn't want the police round. She'd have taken it out on me somehow, she would have confined me to the house.'

They waited for the coroner's inquiry. And when it came, the verdict was suicide.

'I looked at my mother and said, "That was not suicide!" She could not have cut her own throat, not when she was running!'

Millicent re-enacted what she had seen that night. The way the lady held her hands up and shouted, 'No! No! No!' She was still trying to work out whether she was trying to protect her face from more blows, or maybe from the razor that would eventually kill her. She was still trying to work out whether the lady knew what he was about to do.

'She had nothing in her hands to cut her throat with. Even when he punched her, she still had her hands up. You can't commit suicide when your hands are up like this, can you?

'Why did he punch her?' she wondered. 'I never heard any conversation go on. I never heard him say a word. And yet I could hear her saying, "No, no, no, no, no!"

'That worried me for the rest of my life.'

Not long after she was buried, the husband appeared with a 'new lady' on his arm. There was gossip around their township about a possible affair; that he'd gotten rid of his first wife to make way for a second, but no action was taken.

'I was angry,' Millicent admitted. 'I was seething because my mother wouldn't let me speak. She just wouldn't. And my life wouldn't have been worth living if I had of defied her. It was hard keeping it to myself, I felt guilty. There were two or three girls that went missing at that time and their bodies were never found. And the police said, somebody knows somebody who did it. And if they would only talk …'

And so, her regret was born. A regret that would linger, untold, for most of her life.

But like most decisions, there was a reason behind her mum not wanting to go to the police. A reason why she had kept her children so close to home, and herself even closer.

'She was slightly … What would you call it? She had a fear … she had a fear of going out among other people,' explained Millicent. 'That's why she stayed inside so much.

'I had to do all the shopping. If she wanted a pair of stockings, I'd have to go. If she went out to the washing line to hang something up, she'd have her head down, put the clothes on the line and bolt back inside again. A lot of people said they never saw her. If anybody knocked on the door, she wouldn't answer. She had this complex, an inferiority complex.'

Today, that complex would probably be described as agoraphobia, or maybe anxiety, but back then it was a 'complex'. Back then, Millicent knew she had made a mistake the moment she made it. Even as a young teen, she knew that she should have spoken out. And because she didn't, she has been burdened with the guilt of that decision ever since.

It's hard to overrule the people we love. For Millicent, still very young, still living under her mother's roof and by her rules, the idea of going against her wishes must have felt impossible. She was asked to lie by the biggest presence in her life, so she did.

Millicent eventually left home at the age of 18. Her mother's wishes would become less and less important the older and more independent she became. But in that moment in time, on that hot summer's evening and the mornings to follow, keeping to the rules and doing what was asked of her overrode her own instinct to tell the truth. And every time she went back, she'd find herself glancing up at that house with the once-beautiful garden, wondering what would have happened, had she been strong enough to speak up.

'I can't forget it. And I can't forgive myself for not being brave enough to defy my mother. It's too late for me to tell them now. The woman's dead, the man would be dead. I'm the last one left. But if I could have told the police what I knew, that man would have been up for murder. I know it. She did not have the courage to cut her own throat. She was too … she was a timid sort of person, very quietly spoken with a nice little smile. And if you ever went past and she was near the fence, she'd always say, "Good afternoon". But in a soft, quiet way. Never made conversation, just "Good afternoon".

'I've never told anyone else because I don't think they would have believed me. It sounds … It's haunted me for the rest of my life, it really has. It was so dramatic. It's photographed in my memory. I could pick out the house, even draw a sketch of where she ran and where she fell. That's how vivid it is.

'You've no idea how I've woken up with it on my mind. I can hear her, I can still hear her. This is the first time I have broken my silence. Maybe now I will rest in peace.'

Having to Make Hard Decisions

HEATHER

Seventeen years ago, Heather was arrested for murdering her son. But that wasn't what really happened. What really happened wasn't a story of a crime, it was a story of love. Love spotted with hard decisions and regret, and woven so tightly it was impossible to prise them apart.

We arranged to meet outside of her local train station, half a dozen notches along the commuter belt in semi-rural Essex. I arrived on time. And while I waited, I found myself wondering if Heather had changed her mind, but within minutes she appeared in her little hatchback, ready to pick me up. Her pink frosted lipstick was perfectly applied; her snow-white hair cut flatteringly short. We greeted each other with a polite but warm handshake and then she drove us to her home, 10 minutes away. I tried to keep our talk small – the weather, her day – trying to delay all proper conversation until we'd had a chance to sit down.

Heather is 80 now. She is honest and open, and has managed to build a happy, contented life in the aftermath of losing her son, Nigel. But I was nervous about our meeting, worried I would say the wrong thing and upset her. I was yet to discover this wouldn't be an interview, but an opportunity to listen. We settled into her living room, she made us both a cup of tea and then she told me how she helped Nigel die.

Nigel had Huntington's, a genetic, degenerative disease of the brain; it is described as being a mixture of motor neurone disease, Parkinson's disease and Alzheimer's disease. It damages certain nerve cells in the brain and this damage gets progressively worse over time, affecting movement, perception, thinking, judgement and behaviour. Although symptoms can present in children, they usually develop between the ages of 30 and 50, and once those symptoms become visible your life expectancy drops to 15 to 20 years.

There is no cure for Huntington's. And because it's familial, if you have it there's a 50 per cent chance your child will have it, too.

As we started to talk, I settled down on the floor, almost sitting at Heather's feet, wanting to stay close and not miss a word. I glanced at my noted questions and asked the first one on the page, the first of only two I'd end up reading out: What was Nigel like?

She described him as popular and fun. The kid the other kids wanted to be with. He played chess, he loved to draw. She talked about how independent he was, how thoughtful he was. How he always gave people handmade birthday cards and Christmas cards. He sounded like the best of us on a good day, someone easy to love.

At school, he wanted to study Art but his teacher dissuaded him and he ended up working as a sign-writer, then as an engineer for British Telecom. He always had a lot of friends, but as he got older, he started to hold them at a distance.

Heather thinks Nigel knew what was coming.

'He just loved being around people, but if any girlfriends tried to get too close, he wouldn't have it, because he said, "Nobody is going to look after me. I'm not going to let anybody look after me." So that was how he led his life.

'Then suddenly,' she said, 'he was phoning me a little bit more.'

Nigel was thinking about resigning from his job but he was still very young, only in his late 30s, so Heather pressed him for a reason. He reassured her that there was nothing wrong and life kept on rolling.

Then one day Nigel sent his mum a shop-bought card, the first he'd ever given that wasn't homemade. She knew there must have been something wrong and finally, he admitted that he had Huntington's disease and could no longer draw.

He was diagnosed when he was 38. Four years later, he would be dead.

As Heather talked, the thread of what she said looped back and forward in time, picking up the memories she didn't want to forget, the things she wanted me to know about her son – their days out together, their growing friendship – as she circled towards what happened.

'He was beginning to lose his walking,' she explained. 'He was having difficulty swallowing, he couldn't put … at that

REGRETS OF THE DYING

point in time there were VHS videos and he couldn't get his videos in and out to watch. Everything was sort of going.

'He could no longer use a knife and fork either. When we went out, we would eat with our fingers. We did get funny remarks from people, because I did the same as him. Then things got … Nigel was talking about finding ways to die. He'd say to me, "I've been round the train station twice, but I can only think of the driver and I don't want a violent death."'

Heather rushed over the words 'death' and 'die' like they were stepping-stones helping us get to the other side. She leant back in her chair, paused, then continued.

'But always there was this compulsion that he wanted to die. He said to me, "I'm going to stay with my friend for a little while." But I kept phoning and one day he picked up and just said, "Help me."'

By the time Heather got there, she realised he'd been trying to starve himself, using vodka to keep himself unconscious, but he'd run out and was too weak to go to the shop to buy more.

'When he said, "Help me," he really meant, "Go and get me some more vodka." Instead, I called an ambulance and he was taken into hospital.'

Nigel was furious that she'd called for help, but the medical staff got him to start eating again and eventually he went home.

As Heather talked, I noticed her doing something that would be repeated with nearly everyone I met. She stopped looking at me. Her gaze had drifted to a fixed point in the near distance, like she was watching an old movie and was recounting what she could see. With me, but not quite. Then her story came out, like she'd thought it over so many times even the commas knew their place.

It was Nigel's birthday. He was turning 42 and they had planned to spend the day together. She didn't know it would be their last.

'I collected him from the hospital and we were going to go down to Southend but he said, "No, no, I want to go back to my flat." He said, "I like my flat." So, we went back to his flat and I was saying to him, "Well, what shall we get to eat for lunch?"'

Nigel told her not to worry 'about that'. So, she got out her son's birthday cards and presents, but he didn't want those either, saying it was 'too late'. But Heather persevered: 'I said, "I'm going to get your cards out and I'm going to sing Happy Birthday to you."'

Once she finished singing, Nigel told her that his friends had got him 'what he wanted'.

She didn't really know what he meant, but a few moments later he came back into the room holding a packet of 'pink stuff', which she presumed was heroin.

'He said, "They've told me what to do. I put it on a spoon with water and heat it up and put it in the syringe." So, he did that, but his movements were so bad that he didn't get a lot into the syringe and he couldn't inject himself. He was just trying and it was falling on the floor and I was picking it up and giving it to him, and then he looked at me, and he went, "Oh, I can't be bothered with all of this" and grabbed the powder up and swallowed it.'

Nigel said it tasted vile. Heather gave him a drink to wash the vile away, but she could see his movements had become rocky and suggested they lay down.

'So, we lay down together,' she said. 'We talked about his life and we just both went to sleep. Then about three or four hours later I woke up, and I looked at him and I knew he'd nearly gone. His face was deathly white. His lips were bright blue and he only took a breath now and again. I just couldn't stand it any longer. I just thought, this has got to end. So, I picked up the pillow and I put it over his face.

'It wasn't for long, it was only for a very short time. And when I took it off, he didn't breathe again. I sat there with him, I sat there with him for about half an hour and then I called the police.'

A silence fell on the room that neither one of us wanted to break.

My mind flitted back to something Heather had told me – about how resilient Nigel had been. That when he realised he could no longer draw, he would cut pictures out of magazines and create collages instead. And when he could no longer use scissors, he used bits of material. It was like he never wanted to let go of what he loved; like he wanted to keep hold of who he was for as long as possible. But he couldn't hold on any longer. He wanted out, and he chose heroin to help him; a psychoactive opiate that affects the respiratory system and lets your body forget how to breathe.

As Heather was about to speak again, there was a tap on the living-room door. It was her second husband, letting her know he was popping out. It felt like he had sensed his wife was upset and wanted an excuse to check in. She acknowledged him with a quick 'Okay' but her gaze never wavered, like she wasn't ready to leave the moment quite yet. He retreated, leaving us alone again. Heather pulled out a hanky from her sleeve and patted my hand, noticing that I was upset, too.

I asked if she knew what Nigel had planned to do that day.

'I had no idea that his friends had got that for him. I thought we were going out for his birthday, but it didn't take long to adjust to the thought of it, because he wanted it so desperately and he was really happy about it. He said to me, "If you call anybody, I'll never speak to you again." I said to him, "If this works, you'll never speak to me again anyway."

'He said, "This really is a happy birthday."

'We hugged each other and laughed because it just seemed so right. It was right, for him.'

The police interviewed Heather, but at first, she only told them about the overdose. She didn't mention what she had done; she didn't mention the pillow. The following weekend she went back to the police station and amended her statement.

She said, 'I couldn't keep it inside, what I had done, because it was such a big thing. So, I told them that I'd put the pillow over his face. I told them everything.'

Heather was tried at the Old Bailey, the original charge of murder dropped to aiding and abetting a suicide after Nigel's autopsy revealed the pillow didn't really contribute to his death. The judge conditionally discharged her for two years, citing 'exceptional circumstances', and commented that she was 'a brave woman'.

'I can't explain my state of mind at the time,' she admitted. 'He'd tried the train station, he'd tried starving himself. I'd had a few years of him saying he wanted to die and trying to find a way. I knew it would come to it. I just wanted to be there with him, not to actually do it.

'And just to see him lying there, I just felt he can't fail. I thought, it's got to end.'

Heather seemed a bit more relaxed now, relieved to have imparted the worst of it. She picked up her cup, then took us back even further: back to her first husband; how he died, how they met. And how a family secret changed the course of her life.

'He died when he was around 40,' she said. 'Not knowing what it was, he had a lot of wrong treatment. He had electrical shocks given to him and other treatments he should never have had.'

They met through a church youth club. Heather says they got on really well, in part because neither of them came from a particularly steady background: 'So, we sort of bonded in a way and decided we'd like to get married and have our own family. Which we did. He was called Kenneth – Ken.'

Kenneth didn't know he had Huntington's. His dad had had it too, but his mother had buried the facts in various stories about the First World War and nervous breakdowns and psych wards. Heather only found out the truth years later when she was contacted by a man in Canada, researching a branch of his family tree that connected with hers. He shared the fact that he'd been in touch with her mother-in-law, informing her that the disease ran in the family, but was accused of lying and told never to contact her or her children ever again. All of this was confirmed when Heather's solicitor sent her some historic papers after her husband's death and the doctor had written: 'Huntington's disease; family not to be told'.

'I thought that was the doctor's decision,' she said, 'but later on I realised it was her decision, that his mother didn't want them told.'

By the time Heather knew the truth, she and Kenneth already had a family of their own: three boys and two girls. Of their five children, two of their sons, Philip and Nigel, had the disease.

Nigel was 42 when he died. Philip was 50 and had been living in a nursing home.

'We never told Philip about Nigel,' she said. 'We didn't want to upset him.'

Heather recalled a strange moment on the day of Nigel's funeral when Philip suddenly walked up to a glass door and punched a hole in it. She said he didn't know why he'd done it, that he'd never done it before or since, so it felt like he was marking the day somehow.

Because of Heather's arrest, people tend to know Nigel's story better than Philip's. Sometimes when she talked, I had to stop her and clarify which son she was referring to because her mind skipped from one to the other, though the two men sounded very different: Nigel was wildly independent, while Philip liked being looked after; Nigel wanted to end his life and Philip wanted to live as long as possible.

I wondered, given the 50:50 risk of having Huntington's, if Heather and her first husband had known, would they have done anything differently?

Heather paused for a beat, then answered. Her voice once again breaking.

'We probably wouldn't have had children, but then how can I say that I would want to be without them?

'My children have had to grow up knowing what could be in front of them, making the decision that they shouldn't really have children, because it is a dreadful disease. It takes 25 years to kill you, so it's a long, long process and they had to grow up knowing that that could be theirs. So, I said to them, "Look, you've just got to make the best of the life you've got. You've got to do what you want to do, providing you're not hurting anybody else, obviously. But you've got to live your life as you want it, not have any regrets."

'I can't regret that I had the children. I do regret that it's messed up their lives, that it's taken away options they should have had. I do regret that it wasn't a normal family life, but we all did the best we could.'

I was going to ask her about 'that day', the day she insisted on celebrating a birth not knowing a death was already on the cards. But I didn't have to; she was already there.

'I don't have any regrets about what I did, because it was Nigel's wish. He did not want to endure the last years of that disease just lying in bed looking at the ceiling, unable to walk, or talk, or eat properly. That was never Nigel. He would never have done that. And I'm pleased he never went under a train or had a violent death. So, the only thing I regret really is that he never had the chance to have a full life. I think what he did was right for him, and I think I was right to stay with him and help him because he didn't want to die alone.

'Nigel would have loved everyone to be with him,' she noted. 'He would have liked to have said goodbye to everybody, but that wasn't possible.'

I thought Heather's regret would be one clear thing, one moment she'd want to press rewind on and erase. But the things she regretted weren't the most obvious. It wasn't how she felt compelled to help her son, it was another closely related choice she'd had to make years before when her husband was ill.

'I couldn't manage five children and my husband,' she explained. 'He had it quite bad mentally and went into a psychiatric hospital, but his one wish was to come home and I just couldn't accommodate him. He was really upset at not being able to live at home, so you get feelings of guilt afterwards that you never looked after him properly, but at that time it just wasn't feasible. That is a deep regret of mine, but I know that I couldn't have managed him and I couldn't have managed the children. That wouldn't have worked.

'But you still regret it. You still feel guilty about it.

'He used to get very upset at not being allowed to come home. He used to come home and visit, but then when it was time for him to go, I had to call the police and he didn't like

REGRETS OF THE DYING

that. He was a lovely man, he wasn't the sort of person who would hold it against you, but obviously, Huntington's disease changed him and he could be quite belligerent and slightly aggressive. But that wasn't his normal behaviour.'

She recounted a memory to illustrate the bind she found herself in. Of a day when her husband was adamant he wanted to return home to her, so the hospital took his clothes and shoes to stop him from leaving. But somehow, he found a way out of his ward and walked, shoeless, in the snow, for hours before the police picked him up and took him back to safety.

'His one desire was to be at home and I was thwarting that, really ... but I know that I couldn't have managed him. Hard to do actually, but I can't change what happened.

'No, I just had to let it go.'

Heather fell silent, then smiled at me, gently.

Death is a strange thing. It doesn't just take you, it takes the promise of you. When Nigel died, the potential of all that was to follow ended. The relationships, the friends, the fun. All the family gatherings forever marked by that empty seat; that one plate left on the shelf. Nigel was gone, but in a way, he wasn't. He was still present in the way he was remembered; present in the photographs that lined Heather's living room; present every time she retold this story, something she does in the hope she can help legalise assisted dying so that other families placed in the same impossible position won't have to go through the same thing she has.

Heather is from a generation that doesn't necessarily show their affection in a Hallmark kind of way. Meeting her husband was, in part, a practical decision. Having children was expected. But she loved them all without reservation and did what many of us couldn't: she took away her son's pain. And now, nearly two decades on, listening to her talk, the thing that shines through was not only her bravery, but also her love. Not just for her family, but also for herself. She seemed happy – happy for what remained.

Maybe that was it. Heather's secret to dealing with her regrets and the hard decisions that led her there – of her son not living a full life; of not being able to help her first husband – was to focus on what she had, not what she'd lost. To remember all the moments that she had shared with her two sons, and her husband, rather than the memories she would never collect.

She told me: 'I don't see the point of mooning around saying, "Oh, this has happened to me, that's happened to me." I have a good life now. I enjoy the things I do. I think we're fortunate to live in the Western world and I think you have to make the best of what you've got.'

She hadn't drawn a line and simply stepped over it. At some point in the last 17 years, she had decided to live. Not in spite of what happened, but because of it.

Twenty minutes later, Heather dropped me back at the train station, gave a little wave goodbye, then drove away.

I watched as her car disappeared into the distance.

She didn't look back.

Part Five

REFLECTIONS

'Life moves pretty fast. If you don't stop
and look around once in a while,
you could miss it …'

— *Ferris Bueller's Day Off* —

All the Things I Wish I'd Done:
A Letter to Everyone

LIBBY

When Libby tweets, it's prolific. It's 280 characters, dozens of times a day. Sometimes it's a simple post, sometimes it's a longer conversation, back and forth, between her followers and friends scattered across the world. But it's nearly always about family, and cancer, and life. This is where we met: on her timeline, that may only stretch for another year or two.

How do you contact a stranger and ask them to talk about the things that hurt the most?

In Libby's case, you do just that: you ask. Because she talks about the moments that others avoid and does it openly and without apology. So, I asked if she'd be willing to write to me, the way she writes her tweets. Honest, and to the point. She said yes.

So, we began. Talking about all the things she wished she'd done differently and all the things she's learnt and wants to pass on. A letter from her, to you.

Dear everyone,

My name is Elizabeth Joan, but I usually go by Libby. I live in Canada with my husband, my three-year-old daughter, Violet, and five pets (3 cats, 2 dogs).

I am 37 years old and I am dying of breast cancer.

Growing up, I had some limited experience with cancer. My mother began getting mammograms in her forties, the norm at the time. At 48, a screening revealed a 1.8cm triple-negative breast cancer. My mother's treatment was fortunately a success and it never returned. Seventeen years later, on a brunch date in 2019, my sister told me that my father had tested positive for the BRCA1 gene, a gene mutation that can impact your chances of getting breast cancer. This would later prove to be untrue, but the funny feeling I got in my stomach reminded me that I should probably get the lump in my breast looked at again.

The following Monday, I drove to the mammogram clinic with my seven-month-old daughter, unaware this day would delineate my life into 'before and after'.

Most people probably know the numbered stages of cancer: 1, 2, 3 and 4. They have a general understanding that the higher the number, the more fucked you are. Some people also know that Stage 4 is the last one, and that for many types of cancer Stage 4 means 'game over'.

My Stage 3 cancer diagnosis quickly progressed. I am now Stage 4.

When I found out, Violet was sent up to her grandmother's house for a few days while I digested the situation and let my mind mull over the unanswerable questions: Why did this happen? What have I done wrong? Did I do something to deserve this?

In fiction, the protagonist is usually saved at the last minute. It's hard to accept the protagonist in my story will actually die.

I believed breast cancer just did not happen to women my age.

Unfortunately, I learnt it can happen to younger women and that 30% of women with early-stage cancer experience an incurable metastatic recurrence, like me. I also learnt that 70% of breast cancers (including my own) are fuelled by hormones and I would immediately have to enter a medical menopause. And because the hormones from having another baby could cause my disease to progress, I would not be having any more children. Of everything, this forced infertility was the hardest. Receiving this information, just as I was falling in love with my child and motherhood, was a punch in the gut.

People have responded by being really supportive with my diagnosis, but when it's metastatic and ongoing they all just get on with their lives and go away because they don't know how to support someone long-term with dying. Many are just afraid to say the wrong thing. You start to depend more on the friendships of those online who are going through the same thing and become closer with them because they just 'get' it.

I find myself thinking about what I wish I had done.

There isn't much in the way of travel, I have never been a big traveller. I was always working on my career but never seemed to meet the right people, or find the right opportunity to really kickstart things. I wish I could change that so I could feel like I had accomplished something before I die. I wish I had found something that fit me; I feel bad not having a title like 'she's a nurse/engineer/teacher'. I tried teaching for a while but it was so hard to find any permanent opportunities, so I ended up moving around a lot for short-term jobs.

I wish maybe I'd had more insight into myself so I could have found something sooner and not spent most of my 20s and 30s searching for it, just to end up getting terminal cancer instead.

Sometimes I think maybe, if I had known, I would have just partied and did whatever I wanted. My mom and dad were much stricter than the average parents so I was a late bloomer. But I don't know if I would have been happy with myself if I had done that.

I wish I had had kids sooner. I think people are always looking for the 'right time' to do things, especially big things like have children. I think there is never really a 'right' time. If it's something you want, don't delay it because you might never get to do it. If I hadn't gotten sick, I think I probably would have believed I had my kid at the right time, but now I wish I had done it sooner, because it's always something I really wanted and now I don't get to enjoy it in the same way.

I feel sad that I will get sicker and sicker and not get to watch her grow up.

I worry about how the trauma of my death and disease will affect her life. I was a mom for only seven months before cancer took over and I wish I could have enjoyed being a mom without my death hanging over me.

I wish I could have had a second child. That's the biggest thing I would have changed.

I wish I wouldn't have spent so much time with people who made me feel terrible about myself. My last boss was a witch. She was constantly cutting me down or finding ways to make me feel bad about myself. I thought about getting a new job but there has been a financial downturn here in Alberta for the last six years and I could never find the 'right' opportunity, so I stuck it out with her in order to have continuity on my resume. When I went on maternity leave, I planned to find a new job while I was off but I ended up getting cancer instead.

I wish I hadn't given her so much of my life (three years) or allowed what she said to hurt me so much. However, since I did stick at that same job, I ended up getting really good long-term disability coverage, so there are plusses to everything.

I also stuck it out too long with some really bad boyfriends. I wish I could have had the self-esteem to know that and walk away from people who treated me badly. I was pretty and smart and all the things I worried I wasn't. As a kid I always wanted to fit in, but never really did.

I was always kind of awkward. Looking back on my old self, I see how much I had going for me and how important it was for me to love myself, and I wish I could do more of that. If I am around long enough, I hope I can instil in my daughter the ability to see her worth.

If I had more time, I would do something completely different than what I have planned, but I am not exactly sure what that would have been. I think I would try to work on things I was passionate about – like perhaps go back and do the PhD I always thought I would do after retirement from my 'normal' job.

I have lost all the choices in my life. The choice of how many kids to have. The choice of how I look. The choice of which career I want to do. Retirement choices. The choice of the activities I do. The choice of what I put in my body.

The only choice I have left is how I die.

I refuse to use the word 'journey'. Journeys are happy adventures to new places. But I have been granted time to think while I wait for my rogue cells to multiply. My mind has been released from the banalities of daily living and the expectation of planning for a productive and bright future.

Terminal illness takes you so far away from your 'old self' that you are almost able to see yourself from the perspective of another person. I used to be very social and enjoy going out with friends, but my cancer (and embarrassment about the changes to my appearance) have converted me to a homebody. I try to keep busy and sometimes I feel okay, but then I will go through long, low periods when I'm tired and sad and just don't want to do anything.

Loss of my own life is different to other grief. You're basically grieving backwards, because you're grieving something that's going to happen, and once it happens you won't be there anymore. You're going to be dead. It's like my life has been transplanted into a foreign world where everything looked the same but nothing made sense anymore. It's like an alternate universe where my own life is completely destroyed but everyone else's is entirely unchanged.

My mind knows that I will not be saved, that this is truly the end of my life, but denial allows me a thin ray of hope. Denial is a powerful tool. As time goes on this hope is increasingly based on fantasy and speculation, rather than reality. Hope is what we are given when there are no real answers, just probabilities, calculations and luck. The final stage is the 'last hope' stage.

When the hope of living has been destroyed, cancer patients start looking for spiritual hope. During this phase I joined a number of new age groups online. My 'last hope' was that, somehow, I would be reincarnated and granted a new life that I would get to fully live out. Then I began contemplating all the things that could go wrong: what if I was a murderer in my next life, or lived in poverty, abuse or war? What if I was reincarnated and got another terminal illness and had to go through this entire thing again?

I began contemplating that perhaps this life was simply a difficult video game, built to challenge our real selves who lived in a world devoid of struggle.

In some ways it is harder knowing that everyone else's life will continue past the point where mine is. That my presence in my child and husband's life is really a tiny blip. That my loved ones and family will grow and change and develop; think and love and hate and make decisions and all I will do is lay in the ground, slowly breaking down until I am undiscernible from the soil around me.

This realisation makes me feel insignificant.

It feels disappointing. Disappointing that it's pretty much over for me. All the things I had planned for myself while I was healthy are pretty much out the window, and now I'm just planning my will and my funeral. It's hard when I see people doing things I wanted to do with my daughter when she was older, like skiing or attending dance recitals or special occasions, and knowing the likelihood of me being there are so low.

Sometimes, when I allow my mind to wander, I imagine this replacement wife and mother being out there somewhere. She doesn't realise it right now but she has a brand-new life ahead of her, my life, with my people and my pets and my home and everything I've built. I feel angry and jealous that she gets to live the life I have planned.

This person will play such an important role in my child's life, but I won't even get to vet her and decide if I approve. All I can do is hope that she will be able to love my child and fill the spaces I've left behind. Occasionally I feel calm about her existence. I'll be long gone and will not have to see her. In some ways this is easier than experiencing a rough divorce, where I would perhaps have to drop my child off at her house every other weekend. In that alternate universe I would hear her merits and shortcomings, so I am glad I am rescued from any comparisons.

Sometimes I feel furious about her existence. I imagine her having a second baby with MY husband. I imagine MY daughter at the hospital meeting her tiny sibling for the first time and her hopping along beside her dad. I want all that joy to be mine. All the joy of picking a name and producing a clever announcement to slap on your Facebook wall. All of the joy watching a new life. When I allow myself to think about the replacement wife I think this woman is receiving the fallout from my bad luck, but she is also just a woman searching for love and acceptance. I hope I would have liked her.

If I could have my time again, I would make some big changes in how I lived.

I would not live in the future or worry too much about the future; I would live in the positive and assume the best-case scenario was going to happen. I wasted so much time worrying. I worried about so many things regarding my career, etc. and these things weren't ever going to happen. I had a tendency of always thinking the worst would happen and really there is no point living that way because it gets you down. Now that my future is

231

REGRETS OF THE DYING

probably non-existent, I have finally found a way to live in my positive thoughts, but I wish I could apply it to a life story that wasn't so dire.

I would place less value on money and things. We only seem to value our career or the achievements that give us prestige rather than achievements like helping out a friend, succeeding at a hobby or completing a passion project.

Don't let your life be reduced to what you think other people value, or worry about your life being one that other people envy, because in the end the race is only with yourself.

Allow yourself to feel pride in the things you do that do not increase your material status, or move you towards some arbitrary goal – the random acts of kindness, making someone's day and the difference we make in someone else's life are the only things we can truly leave behind.

Be happy with what you have, even if you're always the middle manager and never the CEO. Be happy you got to watch your kids grow up. Be happy that you get to continue to work on your imperfect life. Be happy that you get to be here. Believe me, many people would kill for that opportunity. Money, prestige and power are distractions from the real meaning of life, which is loving and helping others; money should be a means to an end, not the end.

So, if you can learn anything from this dying girl who never truly succeeded at anything, it would be: to slow down, forgive your imperfections, keep working towards your dreams and stop stressing so much. The majority of your problems in life will work their way out. It may not always be exactly what you want to happen, but things can get better.

I would have liked more time, but I'm hoping there is something beyond this.

If there is, I'll meet you there :).

Love, Libby x

Life, Death and Regrets:
A Chaplain's View

JANE & KEITH

Jane and Keith are chaplains. Their working lives are filled with supporting the dying and the soon-to-be bereaved. What they do, day-to-day, is both very similar, but also quite different: Jane is a lay humanist, a non-religious chaplain working out of a busy teaching hospital, and Keith is an Anglican priest in a large hospice. Jane believes in the beauty of the life we have, while Keith believes in a higher power and a life beyond this one.

Given their different founding beliefs, I thought it would be interesting to talk to them separately; to hear their thoughts about life, how people deal with the knowledge that they're going to die, what regrets they may have and the things they want to talk about.

Chaplaincy work isn't usually something a careers advisor would steer you towards, so the first thing we talked about was how they got into this line of work in the first place. For both of them, their reasons were borne out of personal experience.

Jane stepped into the role after retirement; when she saw the job being advertised and remembered a moment, a few decades before, when she was in hospital and the only offer of support for her young son was a religious one. She said that the 'big issue in me pursuing this job was being able to offer choice in a situation where there was none'. So, she decided to be that choice. She's been in the role for over five years now, working across three hospitals with 42 wards. One day she can be spending time in the geriatric ward, talking to older patients, and the next she can be needed on the children's ward, or the emergency department.

Keith entered the world of chaplaincy in 2004. He told me he was already working in healthcare, in head and neck surgery as a maxillofacial technician, when he felt the call to be ordained. But, during the selection process, something happened that really made him reassess what he was doing in all areas of his life: his wife died in a car crash.

'Quite early on at theological college, someone said, "Well, if you look at your life as a jigsaw, what bits are missing? What would make sense? What does that picture look like for the future?" And I thought, actually, healthcare chaplaincy makes a lot of sense for me.

'All these things add up to who we are, don't they?' he said.

And that's what he's been doing for the last 16 years, filling in the bits that were missing: spending eight years in a hospital and eight years at his current hospice, where he heads up the patient family support team.

I spoke to both Keith and Jane at length. Both conversations ventured into many different areas of their work and because of this I have added subject headers to help focus their answers and ease your reading of them.

TALKING

What do the men and women, the young and the old, who find themselves in a hospital or a hospice want to talk about? Listening, and letting people talk is a big part of being a chaplain, but speaking to Jane and Keith, it became clear to me that this isn't just about communicating how we feel; it can also be vital in *what* we allow ourselves to feel.

So, what things take up our headspace as people prepare to say goodbye?

And does talking actually help?

Jane said: 'I find a lot of older people really get something out of telling their story. They seem to really relish the opportunity to tell you about what they did when they were strong and vibrant. Some people have been very fit, right up to a great age, and it can be very difficult to accept the lack of independence and of suddenly being reliant on nurses who are probably the age of their grandchildren for intimate things.

'Hanging on to any kind of dignity,' she said, 'can be really difficult.'

Keith concurred. In his hospice, a lot of time is spent giving people the space to voice their thoughts, regardless of their world view or beliefs: 'With our day-therapy patients we do something called "blether". Blether is a Scottish word for conversation, to while away the time. So, what you do is, you get everyone to write down what they consider to be a big question, or a spiritual question, then everyone in the room has to vote on which one they want to discuss.'

He says it can be anything from the weather to what really matters in life: what really matters in life is probably the most popular.

'I thought,' he admitted, 'when I first heard that question, surely it's to be well? But it's not. Our health is not what matters to most of these people, even though they are sadly dying of something.

'It's about being loved and about having family. Interesting, isn't it?'

He also said that some of the questions were truly brilliant: 'Should our wishes be fulfilled? Does every cloud have a silver lining? Amazing questions, really.'

I asked him what the general consensus to that last question was.

'Well, the guy who asked that question was a bit of a cynic in many ways. He was challenging the whole concept that every cloud has a silver lining and you think, well, actually, what is my silver lining? So, we were able to talk about what good comes out of bad.

'We don't necessarily have to answer it, but just have the discussion.'

FAMILY

Jane and Keith told me that having family and loved ones around you can be understandably important to a patient, but it can also bring its own problems, especially when everyone doesn't share the same model of belief.

'Something that immediately comes to mind,' Jane said, 'is when patients talk about the fact that they have a parent or sister or somebody who is very devoutly religious and they're feeling under pressure to agree to their prayers, or you've got a family member saying, "I keep telling my church to pray for you."

'If it's a loved one, it can be really hard for that person who's dying to say, "Look, stop it. You're actually offending me with what you're doing."'

She said it can be hard when prayers and faith are a family member's way of coping and they're just trying to bring some peace and solace to their loved one, but that it can feel 'really awful when you're terminally ill, having to worry that if you actually say what you want, you'll be upsetting the other person.

'So,' she added, 'sometimes it's about supporting people to say, "This is the end of your life, this is your death, this is about you. If you feel that you need to say something, you say it."' Then she said that this can be a problem from both sides of the divide, whatever the conflicting beliefs are: 'If one person is saying only my way is right and this is what I want you to do, and this is what I'm going to do for you, it completely renders the other person invisible, which is not a good feeling when everybody's trying to say their goodbyes.'

For Keith, the next of kin can also be a sticking point.

'Often,' he said, 'there are families who do not allow the patient the space to have a conversation alone with us, so we have to choose our moment to give them that opportunity. Obviously, it's difficult talking about some of these things when the family are present. But equally, sometimes, we talk more to the family than we do the patient.'

AGE

Does death feel any different, depending on how old you are? I presumed it would – you'd have less time to do all you wanted to; you'd have less time to appreciate and understand the decisions you'd made and why you made them. So I asked Keith: Do people tend to deal with the fact they're terminally ill differently, depending on their age? Do they generally deal with it differently at 45, than at 75, or 80?

From what he'd seen and heard over the years, the answer was yes.

'When you're younger,' Keith said, 'you think you're just invincible. You think death is never going to happen to you. But, you know, it does. Some people will say, "I don't think I'm scared to die, but I'll be a bit miffed if it's this week because I've ambitions and hopes and there's lots of unresolved stuff." Equally, I've come across people in their 90s who have been ragingly angry that they're dying. But that's not common.

'Many people will go, "Well, I've done this, I've done that, I've achieved this, I've achieved that and I feel that I'm ready."

And that's wonderful. But the younger folk,' he noted, 'are just not ready. They've got children they want to see grow up, or they're just retiring, then all of a sudden, a week later, they get a diagnosis and they're just robbed of it.

'Sometimes we're amazed at the way people accept what's happening. We'll try and help them, but of course, telling someone they *need* to accept it is not very helpful. So, yes,' he said, 'it's an ongoing process and the difference in someone's personal circumstances and where they are in life will have a massive effect on how they deal with dying.'

REGRETS

Both Jane and Keith admitted that regrets weren't something that people talked about a lot, but what they did say was very similar: that the regrets you have, just like coming to grips with the fact you're going to die, can depend on your age and at what stage in life you're at.

Jane noted: 'In some ways the regrets are more for your adults in their 40s, 50s and 60s, rather than the people in their 80s and 90s. Forties people are still really quite young, so the regrets are sometimes about having continued to plan for a future that won't happen. I suppose the big difference between really elderly and middle-age people is that elderly people are past the planning stage of their life for the most part, whereas people who are still of a working age often still have plans. I guess everybody kind of feels cheated if they're in their younger years and obviously there's a sadness around those things, not being able to go forward.'

She said it's about not being able to see the next step, about wishing they'd not left things so late, that 'sometimes people will say "I wish I'd learnt XYZ earlier", or "Nobody told me it was going to turn out this way."'

They regret because the time they have left isn't what they imagined it would be and now their plans for the next 10, 20, 30 years may no longer be feasible, or fit into whatever time they have left.

I asked if there was a particular type of person who might regret things more.

'No, I wouldn't say it goes with any particular type of person,' Jane said. 'I mean, the people who have lived, who have actually fully engaged with life in the here and now, do seem to have fewer regrets. The regrets go along with people who wait for things to happen.

'For some people, life is all about planning for the future, they don't actually live in the present. And that, to me, is where the regrets come from.'

When the idea of regrets or wishes unfulfilled does arise, I wondered what they were.

Keith said that in his experience they could be about many things. And like Jane, he also found that people's regrets were often about the plans that were left unfulfilled. That, he said, 'they wanted to do something and they didn't act on it.

'Sometimes, it's really quite sad when people have had a very busy working life and they retire, and they were looking forward to all the things they were going to do or the travelling they were going to do and sometimes people are too ill to ever go and do any of those things. And that, in a sense, is a regret because, had you known you weren't going to get that time, you would have planned some of those things into life.'

Jane returned to the idea of people feeling unable to speak freely, of being too worried to say what they need to say, and how this can leave friends and family with more than 'just' grief to deal with.

'When you think about regrets,' she said, 'it's often the living who have the regrets about what they didn't talk about, about what they didn't say. About whatever connection they didn't take the opportunity to make with that loved one because they daren't talk about it.

'They were consumed with the idea that there's always hope, and if we don't talk about it, maybe you won't die.

'That's where I hear the regrets: what I wish I'd said, you know. What I wish we'd done. Sometimes it's checking out that the other person knew they were loved, or sometimes it's feeling like maybe they never really did understand why I did this, that or the other in life. Things that you think, as the decades roll on, you forget about, and then when that time is very short, stuff starts to come back into focus. And if you don't take the opportunity to live, to have the best time in those last few months ... I think that's another potential for regret: when people find out their hope doesn't keep some-body alive and they haven't taken the time to live.'

Keith told me that Hollywood-worthy bedside regrets are few and far between, but sometimes, for those with an inkling of faith, people occasionally want forgiveness for things that they've done, and sometimes they refer to what they are, but rarely.

'Often,' he said, 'there are issues of regret from relationships. So, for example, people who haven't seen their brother or sister for 15 years and it's been of no consequence, now it is of consequence and they want to resolve that.

'Regrets, I think, spiritually come down to our meaning and purpose. Why are we here? What are we here for? And also, our sense of worth, you know? What have I achieved? Have I been a good father, mother, wife, husband? Have I done a good job?

'I think sometimes there can be a conversation around that.'

WITHOUT REGRET

Sometimes people equate having a regret with having failed. Of failing to live up to our expectation of who we think we are and what we think we want from life.

I know when I ask people about the things they wish they had or hadn't done, at first most people say there aren't any: that they have no regrets. This first reaction is quick, it's knee-jerk, and usually followed by a few things they wish they had or hadn't done, so I wondered what the chaplains thought about this: do we all hold a little piece of regret inside us, untold and unshared, maybe internally explained and rationed away? Or do some people manage to get to the end with a clear score card? And if they do, how do Keith and Jane think they managed to achieve that?

Keith said his feeling was no, but that 'you could have someone who says they've lived a life without regret, when actually, it's almost like they don't care, do you know what I mean? It's a fine line, and I don't want to sound judgemental at all. Equally, I guess you could live a life of great integrity and not regret, if you're able to live up to your own personal expectations.

'I mean, it depends what your hopes are, doesn't it?' he added. 'Whether they're achievable and how your life affects others around you. I suppose it depends on your personality and whether you think you've done enough or not.'

Both Keith and Jane thought that having regrets, and the kind of regrets people have, are subjective. That if you accept that what you did was for the best at the time, then maybe it's not a true regret. And they both agreed that two different people who had done exactly the same thing could view that thing in two very different ways.

'I certainly think it's possible not to be consumed by regret,' said Jane. 'I also think it is possible – with a certain amount of flexibility in your thought, if you're not terribly rigid with everything – to be more philosophical and accept that mistakes are a part of being human. Regretting something says you could have done something differently. But a lot of the time, when people talk about regrets, or talk about guilt, if you really look into it, it's magical thinking that they could have done something differently.'

WHEN PEOPLE SURVIVE

Sometimes when people are told to prepare for the possibility of death, they end up surviving, or living a lot longer than expected. Jane told me that when this happens it can really help put your life into focus. It can allow you to see more clearly what is really important and nudge you towards making changes you may have been putting off, or ignoring, for years.

She said: 'A lot of women have a tendency to defer to their children's needs, to their partner's needs, anything but their own needs. I've spoken to a number of women who, when they have survived a life-threatening illness, become less passive in their own lives. There will be those cases where relationships have held together because it's not a balanced compromise; because somebody has had to suppress their needs to keep the whole thing happy, and if that person comes out of a near-terminal experience and says, "You know what? Life is short and I'm not going to suppress my needs anymore," then sure, that can rock the boat; whether it's a business relationship, a romantic relationship or whatever.

'They start to see that, "Okay, I am actually just as important and I'm not always going to be the one that accommodates everybody else. I'm going to get my voice heard."'

FAITH AND REDEMPTION

Big moments of change can bring us closer to faith or push us further away from it. When I had my brush with death, I went from being a 'quiet' Christian to being a rather devout atheist. But with Keith, it had the opposite effect. His religion, and his beliefs surrounding it, gave him strength when he needed it most. And now, he uses that strength and perspective to help others.

'When my wife died,' he explained, 'I could have taken the view, well, where is God in this? I thought, for me, I know God is there. This awful thing has happened therefore I have to find a way of enabling the two to dwell alongside each other. And indeed, I did. Whilst I don't know why, I now believe stuff just happens, and that God is with us in it and not the cause of it.

'I think for some people, that can be quite revolutionary, really, because I think we live in a world where there's a lot of folklore about faith, which says that good people go to heaven and bad people go to hell. Therefore, as a consequence of that, when something bad happens, some people think it's a judgement upon them. And I think it helps people to say, "No, it's not. You're not being judged for this, it's not that you've done something bad."

'Why do these things happen?' Keith pondered. 'I don't know. But what I do know is that it's possible for people to understand the fact that God is for them and not against them, and it's much better to die in that place than it is thinking you're being judged.'

He said that sometimes patients have a kind of spiritual distress, which happens when someone's worldview doesn't enable them to satisfactorily deal with what's going on: 'It can be all sorts of things, from: this isn't supposed to happen to me; this doesn't happen to me, this happens to other people; what have I done to deserve this? And I thought I had a deal with God.' So, he and his colleagues try and help people recognise why it is that they feel what they feel and then maybe help them to think about things in a slightly different way.

To help them find some peace with what's happening to them.

'So, for example,' he said, 'someone who considers it some form of judgement, we would try to help them to understand that it's not. And indeed, if they have an inkling of faith we would explore that, to see how they view this higher power, or God, or whatever it may be; and see how that can be helpful to them rather than the one who's judging them.'

He explained that it's very difficult to talk about specifics because people are just so unique. But, he added, 'nonetheless, if there is any way of helping people come to a different place, then we'll do that. Some people will say to me directly, "I don't know if I'm ready to meet my Maker." That's good, that's easily solvable. Some of them are unanswerable, imponderable, but you know, we'll do what we can.

'I think for many patients, just the opportunity to talk about things is helpful.'

Keith said there is also 'this thing called redemption. People say to me, "It's all too late," and I go, "Well, no, it's not too late." When it comes to "making good", it is possible for those that believe and trust in God to make things good, to be redeemed. And I think possibly that's why those who reach out to God, at those moments, are able to put stuff to bed.'

And then he expanded on this idea, talking about 'the thief on the cross' and how he couldn't have had any more regrets; that he was dying for the consequences of what he had done and, in that moment, even he was redeemed.

'That's exactly what happens for some of those folks who have regret. And in absolving someone, if that's what they want and that's what they believe and trust is happening, then that can help.'

Jane doesn't believe there is a god, or a 'higher' being, but she repeated Keith's observations when it came to speaking to someone with faith.

'Sometimes,' she said, 'there might be the, "Oh, what did I do wrong? Why is God punishing me?", this sort of thing. If it's a person who doesn't believe in God, obviously they're not saying that, but there will still sometimes be the "Why me?" response. "Have I done something wrong?" or "Did I do something to deserve this?", which is quite common initially.'

She added that sometimes people presume if you don't believe in God then you haven't thought through your beliefs; that non-religious people are seen as having no belief system at all, which isn't really true: in fact, she thinks that sometimes they can develop a more robust set of morals to live by, because there is no list of rules or text to follow; they have to be fully thought through and decided upon, person to person.

And when it came to those people who are dying, she said: 'They're certainly not welcoming their death, but by the time it gets there, I have found non-religious people to be quite accepting.'

HOPE

Hope was also a subject that came up a number of times, with both Jane and Keith.

Hope can be a very positive thing, something that helps us through the toughest of times, but I've also heard many stories of how hope can stop people from accepting the reality of what lies ahead.

'It's something that I've heard from patients,' said Jane, 'where family are urging them to fight on, "Let's do this one more treatment, let's keep going! There's always hope!" and the patient is saying to me, "I am exhausted, I have nothing else to give, I've fought as far as I can fight. I just want to go now." And of course, they can't say that openly to their family member because they're terrified it will look like they're giving up and will leave them even more upset.'

I brought up the story of Mike, a man I was briefly pen pals with. He was on death row in America, and after 27 years of legal stays was finally executed in 2017. I remember him talking about the idea of hope – something that has always had a positive connotation in my own head – and how it had become a negative for him. Because when he expected nothing or prepared for the worst, he wasn't let down. But, when I spoke to him, decades into his sentence, he said that hope, and feeling hopeful about his chances of living or being exonerated, made every day harder to cope with.

I wondered: if you were dying and found yourself surrounded by people expecting you to be hopeful, could this be detrimental for the person at the heart of it, trying to cope?

Jane said, 'If people don't accept time is limited and now is your opportunity to say the things you don't want to leave unsaid, whether that's the patient or whether that's the family, and we're into the realms of "Ooh, no, let's not talk about that. Hope, there's always hope, there's always hope," I always think, "No, there isn't, and you're wasting time", you know?'

I shared this with Keith, and once again, he was in agreement.

'You get people who are prepared to go. And their family is going, "No, don't say that, don't say that." The patient themselves is accepting of what's happening and yet those around them are not allowing them to come to that place of acceptance. And we have to come to a place of acceptance.

'It's so cruel, isn't it?' he added. 'It's not humane.'

But, with all that said, he still felt that hope had a role to play. Maybe not at the very end of things, but as part of a gradual letting go.

'Misplaced hope is a disaster,' he said. 'But hope is important. And I think our hope shifts as things go on.' He has noticed that hope progresses through a series of stages: you go to the doctor's and you hope it's nothing serious and then when you find out that it's serious, you hope you will still have a long life.

'We shift our hope on,' he added. 'And eventually, if we do that, for those that can, their final hope is to have a peaceful end. But it takes time, and if people haven't got that time, then often they can't get to that place.'

DYING

Those final moments as life comes to an end can be scary and overwhelming to the person who is dying, and to all the loved ones around them. We worry that they are in pain; that they're distressed; that we haven't said all that we needed or wanted to say.

I asked what this moment is like: Jane, being a humanist chaplain, says it's something she rarely sees because when people call for support at this late stage, it's usually to perform a religious ritual, like the Last Rites. But, on the odd occasion she is present, she said that rather than just sitting there in silence, she asks if there are any poems, readings or books they really enjoy and she will read to them.

'I haven't met anybody who hasn't actually really focused on the value of their life,' Jane told me. 'Some people cope with it by pretending it's not happening. Some people actually say, "I don't want to know the details, I don't want to know my prognosis in terms of how many months I have left." They cope with it that way and they carry on as best they can, not thinking about it. For other people, they get comfort out of making all the plans.

'So much of it depends on the individual.'

She explained that death, for some, can come quickly, but for others, it can take time.

'That last visit,' she said, 'whether it is the patient themselves or the other people there, can be so long and lonely. Nobody can predict the moment it will happen. And getting over that fear and seeing a way through without feeling a load of guilt if it happens when you weren't there at that exact time is important.'

Keith talked about this, too: the worry of people dying alone.

About how the next of kin can be sitting bedside and the moment they leave their loved one alone, they slip away. Most of us will probably know friends or family who have experienced this and seen the guilt and worry it can leave in its wake: if only they hadn't left the room, if only they had stayed …

During Keith's many years as a chaplain, he's come to realise that this might not be down to bad luck or timing, but a subconscious decision by the dying to be alone at the end.

'Sometimes when you step out of the room after keeping vigil for days, or weeks, and then they "go" – it's because they want to die in private. That they feel ready. I often warn families that for many patients, for many individuals, those final moments are very personal and in fact they will wait until there is no one in the room.'

He said that the guilt the surviving family and friends can feel in this moment of aloneness can be misplaced because 'they never were going to be there. For some patients it's quite a deliberate ability to decide that that's their moment to go. And I will say to the families, it's because they are assured of your love and they know you're there.

'Everything is resolved, therefore they're free.'

Sometimes family members ask Keith to stay with them and perform some end-of-life prayers. He says that when someone is in the last stages of life that death is not a failure, it is the goal, 'to ensure that this individual from that moment on had a good death in the company of his family'.

It's obvious that Keith and Jane both take their roles very seriously but I wondered how it felt when your work is full of the big questions of life and the deep unknowns of death. I wondered how they managed to do what they do and then go home and watch telly, and mow the lawn, and live without feeling the weight of other people's loss and grief. And if there's anything the rest of us can learn from their ways of coping.

'Dealing with death does leave its mark on you,' Keith admitted. 'However good you are, you become tired. It can become wearing and I think you can have a slightly distorted view of life, this life. Death becomes more commonplace, I suppose, which it is.'

All chaplains, no matter what environment they work out of, have to take part in supervision – a window of time where they get to talk to someone about their workload and patients. Keith uses his regular supervision to make sure he hasn't become numb to it.

'I think it's worth just asking that question of yourself, that I've not become so accepting of death,' he said, 'even though it is part of everyday life. Frequently, I've come across chaplains, who go, "I just need to do something else now."'

He added that he thinks dealing with death and grief affects your personal ability to function at some level, so he likes to officiate weddings and minister in other contexts to make sure the amount of life vs death he's dealing with is a bit more even: 'When I was in the bereavement follow-up service in my previous role, I was learning four new ways to die every week. That wasn't helpful. At least I find the focus of this work at the hospice is much better in that regard.'

'I cope with it,' Jane explained, 'by knowing that it makes a difference to be there for that person. I don't want to come across as somebody really cold and matter-of-fact. Everything does touch me, but through life you learn to not let it tear you apart, otherwise you couldn't do the job.' She admits it takes a fair bit of practice to remain empathetic and 'not switch that part of yourself off without being absolutely gutted by it every time; you just could not survive.

'And, I guess,' she added, 'that is the thing that sustains me: knowing that this person must go through what they're going through regardless of whether there's anybody there to help them or not. So, being able to be there for them, it almost feels like it gives me a foundation to stand on, so I'm not lost in swirling emotions. That my focus is wholly on them and not how I'm feeling.

'I might reflect on it later and feel really sad. That's a big part of the job, making sure you reflect on it. That's one way you don't lose your empathy and maintain some balance. I've been sad with patients but it's always really, really important not to let your stuff take over. Sometimes that can be very connecting, but there's a risk if you start crying then they start looking after you and I wouldn't want that situation.'

She said that sometimes that can be a bit more difficult at a funeral and recalled one service that she found particularly hard. It was for a baby and the mourners were all dressed like 'stereotypical tough-guys', in casual black clothes and dark sunglasses: 'Because of the way I was standing and the way the sun was coming through the window, I could see behind their glasses, the tears rolling down their faces. And to see somebody who is fighting to hang on to their emotions …

'I really get it,' she said, 'how fragile life is. There are no guarantees for anybody, therefore I am going to engage with every day, live every day and really sort out what is important.'

Keith said that if he gets to 85, he'll think he's done well, because 'you live in a world in which everyone dies much younger than that. But then equally, you also make the most of today. That's the other side of that coin, you know.

'You don't put things off till tomorrow, you make the most of today.'

WHEN WE DIE

What happens when we die? Is there a heaven and hell? Is there an afterlife, or a 'better' world? What, if anything, comes next?

In reality, the answers to these questions are unknowable but that doesn't stop them from being things that most of us, at some time or another, have contemplated. And they are the questions where Keith and Jane's answers were, understandably, the most different.

Keith said: 'I think as a Christian there is some sort of life beyond, where there is no more death or dying or pain or tears. I cannot imagine what it's like, because we are told …'

And then he quoted a scripture from the Bible (1 Corinthians 2:9) to illustrate his point:

No eye has seen, no ear has heard,
and no mind has imagined

what God has prepared
for those who love him.

'So I think it's okay to live with that mystery,' he said. 'But yes, I do think there is something beyond. I think that we are all just travellers here.'

He used an analogy about books from C.S. Lewis to explain this idea: that if the life we are living is the cover and the title, then the story inside is 'what lies beyond'.

'Whether we think we are created or not,' he added, 'we are here on this planet in the middle of the universe, this little dot, and I think we're here essentially to be the best that we can be.'

Jane offered no analogies or scriptures. Logic, science and humanity guide her humanist view that there is nothing beyond 'this' – no second chances, no heaven and hell. No reincarnation that some religious groups subscribe to. She believes that there is nothing but the here and now and in that lies the value of life.

'I think that when we die it's "lights out",' she told me. 'We stop. Our conscious self or any other way of defining ourselves stops. We do not exist just as we did not exist before we were born. The only way we continue is in the memories of the people who knew us when we were alive.'

HOW TO LIVE A GOOD LIFE

Near the end of my conversation with Jane, we talked about all the things she'd learnt after all her years of listening. One of the questions I've been thinking about throughout my many

REGRETS OF THE DYING

meetings was the opposite of having regrets. Not being regret-free, but being able to look back with contentment rather than a flowing list of should have, could have, would haves.

So, I asked her, in her experience, how do people create a happy, contented life?

'Being true to yourself,' she replied. 'And that might mean learning about yourself, so that you know what you have to be true to.

'Balance would be one word I would come back to. Not that you have to stay balanced all the time but being able to regain your balance, being able to come back to that calm, centred place is a great part of happiness.'

She said she's not Buddhist, but there are things that she likes about some of the Zen philosophy and the idea of not chasing happiness. 'Happiness,' she said, 'is too vague a goal. When people say to me, "Oh, I just want to be happy," you say, "What does that look like, then?" Some people can't name it. It is such an illusion. But, liking who you are, learning to accept disappointment, to not look for instant gratification: all of those things contribute to this sort of overall contentment.

'And flexibility,' she added, 'because the idea of being made of steel, that's actually not the best way to be strong: having some flexibility is.'

She compared this idea of rigid strength with the materials used to build skyscrapers, and how it didn't take long for builders and architects to discover that if you built very, very tall buildings that were absolutely rigid, they were at greater risk of collapse.

'Your strength isn't necessarily in this tougher-than-steel rigidity. It's when you can flex with the environment, with the things that life brings you and adjust to it. So much after that depends on the individual. So, the best way, as far as I can see, is to live every day to its fullest.

'That doesn't necessarily mean being happy all the time, but it does mean being engaged in life. If you have a perfectionist attitude then you're very much more likely to have a lot of regrets. But if you have that flexibility, are philosophical when things go wrong and accept that that is also part of life, then you're much less likely to see them as regrets.'

No Regrets

SIMON

Simon Ricketts was a journalist. He had a loyal following online, a truly magical way with words and a passionate love of football and politics. When we talked, he was 48 and terminally ill with a cancer that had started in his colon and spread to, as Simon put it, 'my stomach and my pancreas, and dotted elsewhere, hanging around inside me like violent gangs at a series of darkened bus stops.'

When I heard about his prognosis, I got in touch to see if he would like to talk. His reply? 'I would be interested but I do wonder if I would be right for it. The reason being, I don't think I have any regrets.'

I couldn't quite get my head around this, especially given how young he was.

I wondered what 'having no regrets' actually meant to him. To any of us. Can we really live through decades of decisions and not find ourselves rethinking any of the choices we'd made? Is that realistic, or maybe just a coping mechanism? A denial of how we really feel because we know that we may have run out of time to change things? And what about all the other people I'd talked to: if Simon had no regrets, then why did they?

So, I sent him a handful of questions – about regrets, about being diagnosed and what it feels like, knowing you are dying – and, like a true journalist, he recorded the answers on his phone. This is a transcript of those recordings.

WHAT DO YOU REGRET?

I've thought about this question, I've thought about what I regret.

These kinds of things come to you when you obviously start to take account of your life. And I can honestly say I don't regret anything, I really don't. Regret for me suggests something that you wish you hadn't done and because you wish you hadn't done it, it kind of lives with you and colours your life. Something that has hung around for a long time. I don't have any of those things. I don't.

There's a phrase in Italian art called *pentimento*, which I found out about a while back. It means an alteration to a painting. Like these old paintings that they examine and find previous sketches or previous paintings underneath or even the same painting but an alteration. It struck me that we're all kind of like these paintings and we grow and alter as time goes on and we may improve parts of ourselves, we may not improve parts of ourselves, but we are always changing as people and therefore regret, for me, is not something that I hold on to.

I could obviously regret having cancer, but I don't regret anything I did, because I like to think that if I managed to hurt somebody or upset somebody, I either had to, or I've redressed the hurt: I've apologised or I've made amends in some way. Any mistakes I've made I've tried to redress them, but I don't hold regrets with me. I don't hold them at all.

I believe everything that you do is part of who you are and as long as you feel like you did whatever you did for the right reasons and for the proper reasons, for good reasons, or for at least positive reasons, then I don't regret anything.

WHAT DID IT FEEL LIKE BEING TOLD YOUR CANCER WAS TERMINAL?

One of the worst things about having a prognosis of terminal cancer or any kind of fatal, terminal disease, in my experience, is knowing that you're going to have to tell people.

You know, the doctor told me and that's it. I'm one person. But there are scores of people who love me and care for me, and I was going to have to look them in the eye and tell them: my mother, my brother. My girlfriend was there at the time and I was worried how she would react. I'd actually warned her beforehand, if the news is bad, please try not to burst into tears. Because I'm a very factual person, I wanted to know how long I'd got, how it was going to kill me, you know. What the next steps were.

I was sat on a chair, there was a doctor in front of me and a Macmillan nurse, which gave me a clue that the news was going to be bad, and my girlfriend was there writing down any notes. My immediate feeling was just utter paralysis, but if I'm honest, I had kind of expected it or I had kind of feared that the cancer would not go away and that it was back and that it was bad.

I was thinking in that kind of scientific-y way, but the thing that strikes you immediately is that I've got to tell people and they are going to be upset and I am going to be responsible for making people cry; I just thought of the people I was going to have to tell. And I hate to make people sad and I hate to make people feel upset.

The weird part of my current situation is that when I was younger, when I was a teenager, I was convinced I was going to die before I was 40. I had a strange feeling of … I don't know, a premonition or whatever. It's one of the reasons I didn't learn to drive straightaway, because I was convinced that it could probably end up with me having a fatal car crash. I wasn't morbid or, you know, obsessed with it.

I was just convinced that I wasn't going to make old bones.

HOW DO YOU COPE, KNOWING YOUR TIME IS LIMITED?

I sometimes panic about time running out, but then that initial burst of: Oh my God, I'm going to die, that comes early on, or it did with me. So, one of the first things I did was make sure my Will was up to date, make sure my affairs were in order, and make sure that I wasn't leaving anything behind that would just be too much hard work to sort out. I want to make it as easy as possible for everyone when I'm gone.

In my mind, I run on two tracks. One of them says I've got six months to live, so I've got to enjoy what I'm doing and be prepared for the fact that I could be gone in six months. The other track in my mind is that I will go on for a bit longer than they expect, maybe two years, three years, I don't know.

So, I budget in my head, if you like, for both occurrences, but what I don't do is worry about missing something. It could be easy for me to say I would love to see my niece, who's 12, get married. Or I'd love to see something happen or I'd love to … you can't do that.

One of the things that this kind of diagnosis does is it makes you just enjoy what you have, what you've had and what you're having every day. That you're breathing. I make a joke about it but I can just breathe in now, and I can breathe out, and that is a miracle that you can do that. You are a growing, living, human thing and you do – it gets a bit existential, but you do find yourself just marvelling at the fact you're even here, marvelling at the world around you, just being grateful for that. But also, every now and then you get a jolt. You might wake up in the night or you might be drifting off, daydreaming during the day, and then suddenly you realise or you remember and it comes back with a fairly sharp jolt that you're dying, you have terminal cancer and you won't be around for a long time.

But that knowledge is in a weird way liberating because so many of us don't know that we're going to die, or we don't know when or we don't have any kind of inkling that we could be dead in the morning. So, once you've faced up to the fact that we're all dying and we all have a finite time, there's a liberation to it and you can say things you want to a bit more and you can do things that you want to a bit more. And people can say things to you that they want to because they know that time is limited. Time is limited for everybody. But when you get a little bit of a deadline, even if it's a fairly woolly deadline, then you start to prioritise a bit more.

HOW DO YOU LIVE A LIFE WITHOUT REGRET?

There's no kind of secret, but I do think that you should correct your mistakes. I think you have to accept your weaknesses and know that you do things sometimes that aren't the way that other people want them to be done. Whether you change them or not, that's up to you, but for me, accept the things you're weak at and try to learn to live with them and try to – it's an old cliché as well – but try to own them, don't deny that you're bad at something. Just accept it and try to either be better at it or just accept that you're bad at it and make allowances for the fact you're bad at it, and try to explain that to others.

Knowing yourself, I think, is an incredibly important part of life anyway and it takes time to get to know
yourself. You start out being a person that you think you
should be. You sometimes try and be a person that you
think others want you to be, so I think knowing yourself,
knowing what you enjoy, what turns you on, what makes
you go, what gets your heart beating, that's important,
and I would always suggest that to anyone: write down
what you're good and bad at, what you like and what you
don't like, what you don't like about yourself, what you
like about yourself, and just accept it, because we're all
flawed, aren't we?

We're all weird little blobs of flesh that make errors.

That's really it. The only thing about having no regrets
is to try and obviously live an error-free life, which you
can't do. But my overriding thought is to try always to be
kind. Try to be kind to people. It's so much easier than
being nasty. Well, actually, it's not easier, it's harder. It's
harder to be kind to somebody but it's better.

Being nasty to people for no reason, for no provocation,
for no motive – for me, being nasty seems like a rusty way
of living. Yes, there are times when you want to shout at
somebody who's cut you up in the road or been impolite to
you in work or something, but go harder. If you go harder
at being nice, I find it makes my life so much happier.

I treat it very much like a bank account. Life is, if
you like, a karma bank account and if you pay in more
than you take out then really you can have a much happier

night's sleep than if you're forever being nasty or forever trying to do somebody down or trying to misbehave or put one over on someone. Oy, what a life. I couldn't face it!

WHAT IS THE SECRET TO LIFE?

I don't think there is a secret to life. I think the secret to life is you're lucky to have it.

Life is for living, if you like, in a very straightforward way. Life is an incredible thing, whether it's a human life or a plant or an animal's life, it's an incredible thing.

I think the point is to enjoy it as much as you can. Some people find that difficult and some people's circumstances make it difficult, but as somebody who's as lucky as me, then I'm going to make damned sure I enjoy it.

That's really it. Enjoy your life. Try to make it something that others enjoy as well. If you can help other people enjoy themselves, for me that's what it's about.

LAST QUESTION: HOW DO YOU WANT TO BE REMEMBERED?

I don't think it's really up to me to decide how I'm going to be remembered.

I could be remembered by lots of people in lots of different ways, but I suppose if I was asked, if I wished to be remembered in a certain way – I suppose just fondly, just with kindness, you know, as someone who paid in more than they took out in the bank account of life. And yes, someone who's loved and someone who has been loved. Someone who *is* loved. I think love is a very important thing in people's lives, whether it's family love or relationship love, or even just friendship love.

I think love is very important and the feeling of contributing to others' happiness and not just happiness, contributing to their kind of sense of being connected to you.

That's really all that life, to me, is about.

The connections you make with people and the happiness you bring but also the strength and support you bring, and the feeling of being someone worthwhile in somebody's life. It's a nice feeling.

As Simon segued from thoughts about the 'strange liberation' he felt knowing he was going to die, and how we all need to find a way to be happy, I realised he wasn't in denial. He wasn't running away from the fact he was dying and he wasn't papering over the cracks: he really did have no regrets. And it wasn't because he'd lived some perfect life. It was because he lived his life with a very simple, but deeply held, philosophy: that if you apologise and make amends for your mistakes then you can't really regret what you did, or said, because you probably had a good reason for doing it at the time. And that those mistakes, those missteps, are what make us who we are.

On 29 December 2018 a post appeared on Simon's Twitter account, announcing that he had died. He was 50 years old. These were his last words to the online world:

Now my time has come to an end and I will be departing. Not just the newsroom, I'm sorry to say. My illness means I am leaving for good. This terminal cancer has lived up to its name and will be seeing me off very soon.

I will be leaving the building but I won't have the carriage clock. That's something I can't be happy about. What I can be happy about – what I can hope is – at some near time in some near place, even if it is inside your minds, some of you will have a little 'banging out' ceremony for me. I'd really like that.

If you do, then make it loud. Keep the noise up. Just for a little bit.

What I've Learnt:
10 Tips to Live a Less Regretful Life

(IN NO PARTICULAR ORDER)

When I started all this, I was in search of answers. Answers to why we regret, what we regret and how we could maybe regret a little bit less.

I was in search because I was overtaken by it, I was consumed.

I felt so much regret for the things I'd done, or *not* done, over the years and for the decisions I'd made. Regret for not being in the body I wanted, for not having the career I had imagined I'd have; for not being the kind of person I thought I would be by now. For spending so much of my energy and focus on trying to have another baby. For being in a marriage that no longer made me happy.

For wasting time. Way too much time.

I was 37 when I nearly died. As I write this now, I'm nearer to 50.

I have lived over a decade longer than I could have. I've had more than 10 years' worth of life I nearly didn't get to experience. That realisation didn't change me overnight, but

I do feel changed now. Listening to so many different people talk about their lives has been a revelation. It felt like the more I listened, the more their decisions – and my own – made sense.

They taught me that we do what we do for many reasons: because we lack the confidence or the financial means; because we haven't yet learnt the lessons we need to learn in order for us to make a different choice; because we were trying to right the wrongs of the past; and because we were simply doing what we thought was best at the time.

They also taught me that, over the years, I'd discounted the everyday moments of joy and all the things I'd actually done, and focused solely on my unticked to-do list.

They made me realise that the anonymity I'd always felt, the invisibleness of being a bit plain, of being a bit ordinary, all the things that (in my mind) had stopped me from achieving were actually my superpower. That I didn't need to make some grand gesture towards a new and magical life, I just needed to be myself and learn how to appreciate the everyday.

And they made me see that I had a view of who I thought I was, and where I wanted to be, and because I wasn't 'there' yet (wherever 'there' was) I deemed myself a failure.

Basically, I realised I had been wrong about so many things.

I also came to realise, after listening to everyone being so honest and open about their lives, that it was time that I was honest about mine. It was time that I actually listened to myself; to what I really wanted and what I didn't. And that I really had to make some major changes.

The main one was that my marriage was over and it had been for a very long time.

It was a very hard decision to leave our relationship after 22 years together, but it was the right one. I hadn't been happy for years, neither of us had, but the idea of saying 'I'm done' just felt too daunting. I was a stay-at-home mum; I hadn't made a liveable wage for years and I had lost all confidence in myself. My ex-husband is a very good man and an amazing father, but us, together, no longer worked.

When Sid explained what love was, he told me: 'When you get it right, the cogs fit.'

We tried and tried, but our cogs no longer fitted. It was like they were running on two different systems, independently working but not actually connecting or helping each other.

Eventually we both came to the same conclusion: that it was time to move on. That we had just done the best we could, with what we had and what we already knew.

And that's the trouble with regrets. We look back at the act or moment we wished we could undo, but not the things that led up to it.

We don't look at the real reasons behind the reasons.

We look back and chastise ourselves for our choices and decisions, or we look ahead to the things we may never have. We live in the yesterday and tomorrow, but never today. We look back with, as Jane put it, a head full of magical thinking; telling ourselves that all we had to do was make a different decision at a few select moments and then everything else would have been different, too. It may have been, but in reality, there is no way of really knowing that.

And that lack of focus for the present day is the reason why we keep gathering more and more regrets. Because while we're looking back, and forward, time marches on. And time, like love and childhoods, goes by so quickly. It feels like one moment we're looking forward to some bright, far-off future full of holograms and hoverboards, and the next we're knocking on 30, or 40, or 50 and wondering what we've been doing for all these years.

Music you used to dance to and fall in love to is now considered retro, or – even worse – vintage. If you have children then you will probably have already become the embarrassment that your parents were to you.

But how did we get here? How can we feel the same but look so very, very different?

One minute we're young with a wide path of possibilities in front of us and a host of choices to make, and as the years trip by, our path narrows. Sometimes we regret what we've done in the past, because we see the future as a place of limited possibilities. Because it's easy to think, this is it. That where your life is right now is where your life will always be. That what is left is just a long, straight road in front of us. But we do still have choices to make, no matter what age we are.

They didn't go away, they merely changed focus.

They may not be the huge tentpole moments of life – decisions about children, money, education, your ambitions or career – but they can be just as important. They are about what you want to fill your days with, who you want to share those days with, and whether you're truly content with where the paths you've already chosen have taken you.

They are about looking at what you have right now and asking yourself: Am I happy with the life I am living? Is there anything I want to change? Are there things that I will regret if I don't do them while I can?

Are there things you have come to like and need to learn to appreciate a bit more?

The regrets you hold in your hand right now are all very different, but there is a pattern to them – a set of reoccurring themes not only in the kind of regrets people have, but also in the types of situations that can lead us to have those regrets in the first place. So, as I've spent so much of my life writing lists, I've written one for you now: a list of the top 10 tips to live a less regretful life.

1. DON'T LIVE IN THE FUTURE.

Life, family, ambition – they all need planning. But if you live too much in the future, if you plan too much and things don't work out, the effect of that perceived failure has the potential to hit you much, much harder than if you'd taken the time to enjoy what's happening right now.

This is something I have done a lot over the years – planning rather than living. Everything I did was viewed in the rear-view or some distant future. I planned and I scheduled, but none of it made me happy, because in the process of thinking back and looking forward, I forgot to enjoy the present.

Unfortunately, I'm not alone in this.

Both Keith and Jane said this is something many of the people they speak to regret, especially those who find themselves with a life-limiting illness at a younger age. That we think we'll have time, and by the time we realise we don't, it can be too late.

Libby wished she'd been able to have another child; she wished she'd achieved more in her work-life. She had plans for her future, but now she knows there is not enough future left.

Living in the future is something we all have to do to a certain degree, so it's unrealistic to think we can only live in the moment. Maybe what we need to do is make plans, work towards our goals, but remember: today is worth as much as tomorrow. Value it.

2. BE HONEST ABOUT WHAT YOU WANT.

What do you want from your life? What do you want your life to be? Do you want to be in a relationship, or would you prefer to be single? Do you want to have a family, or be child-free? Do you want to travel the world, or focus on your career?

What do you need from the people who love you? What do you need from yourself?

Jo wanted her parents to get her brother the help he needed and for them to create more of a stable home. She told them but they didn't hear, so everything just continued: her dad being emotionally erratic, her mum relying on others to look after her and Jo being caught in the middle. She now wishes she'd made her feelings more clearly known, she wishes she'd got them to get help for her brother and that she'd made her mum realise what her dad had put them through.

Sid regretted not staying in contact with Lilias. He wished they'd found a way to be together, but he knew his father didn't approve, so when it came down to it, when he was on the brink of starting their life together, he let it drift. He just disappeared.

He wished he'd explained what had happened to their flat and how he wanted to find a way to be together. But he didn't and now, 50 years on, he's still trying to put his 'ghosts to rest'.

It's hard getting people to listen, just like it's hard telling them what you really want. But the answers to all of these questions – to who we want to be with, to what we want to do and where we want to live, and more – are the building blocks of our lives. They are the doors, the windows and the walls to everything else. Be honest about them or you'll end up living a life that will never truly feel like home. Which leads us to …

3. REMEMBER THAT WHAT YOU WANT MAY CHANGE, AND THAT'S OKAY.

Most of us live between some kind of bracket – of spouse, best friend, boss, partner – labels that connect us to our relationships, our abilities and to who we are as human beings. They can make life seem clearer, but if they are incorrect, or if they have become incorrect over time, they can tie us to the past and not the future.

Because what we want, what gives us joy, is forever changing. The things that made us happy at 21 are rarely what we need or want at the age of 42. Sometimes we have to learn to let go or risk living a life that no longer fits.

Kathy had wanted to leave her marriage for years, but she was worried about splitting up her family, and worried about being on her own; so she stayed, hoping that things would get better. She had entered into their marriage with the very best of intentions, but deep down she knew that her second husband wasn't enough and that she had changed her mind.

It took Kathy 36 years to admit how she felt and leave. She regrets that now – she regrets the amount of time she spent trying to improve what she had, rather than freeing herself to find contentment on her own, or to discover a relationship that could have really given her all that she was searching for.

Sometimes we shy away from change because it can be seen as a sign of failure. A sign that we've made a bad decision, or that we couldn't commit. We are taught that failure is something to be ashamed of. But it isn't.

Everything has a lifespan and staying in a situation that no longer makes us happy or content can be more of a failure than leaving and moving on.

Splitting up or getting a divorce isn't (always) a failure. Changing jobs, downsizing, upsizing, giving up a dream we may have clung onto for years – like having a baby, or getting a promotion – doesn't always mean that we've failed. Changing and recognising the dream you once had no longer has a place in your life is a good thing. A very good thing, in fact. Because it allows you to make space for something more positive.

To leave a relationship that no longer works, to say goodbye to a friend who always lets you down, to let go of a career that no longer brings you joy or fulfilment – these aren't the worst things that can happen. Change isn't the worst thing that can happen. It might shake you for a while, it might be scary and unknown, but if what you have right now isn't making you happy, what are you really losing if you give it up?

4. REMEMBER, YOU CAN'T ALWAYS BE IN CONTROL.

Sometimes our regrets are borne out of the difference between the life we imagined we'd have and the life we've actually ended up living: when we thought we'd have kids and we haven't; when we thought our relationship would be full of love, and it isn't; when we thought we'd be the one running the company and we're still the one running the errands.

But most of us live in a less than perfect world. Sometimes we have to make decisions that are compromised and influenced by things outside of our control.

Anonymous regretted not being there for their son as he was dying; Charli regretted the last words she said to her brother, James; Heather regretted not being able to have her first husband living back at the family home as Huntington's disease tightened its grip on him.

All of these regrets are different but also very similar, because they all came out of situations they weren't able to control.

Anonymous's regret was very clear and present but, in reality, they were simply trying to do their best in an impossible situation. They had no control over the fact that their son had cancer. They had no control over the fact that they had a cold and could be contagious. The only thing they could have controlled was making the decision to defy medical advice and going to visit him, but that could have resulted in his treatment being halted, or worse, cancelled. They had no idea that would be the last chance they had to see each other. They had no idea, they just did what they thought was best, out of love and care, not out of selfishness or neglect. Anonymous had no way of knowing, so they made the best decision they could with the information they were given. It was not their fault.

Charli regretted those last words to her brother, James, telling him, 'Don't come back again' after forgetting his keys for the umpteenth time. But she had no way of knowing what would happen that night. She had no idea that she would never get to speak to him again. She wasn't riding that bike; she wasn't letting her brother ride it. The circumstances of his crash were out of her control. All she could do was deal with the aftermath.

Tom regretted letting his health slip and becoming morbidly obese. He seemed to see it as a sign of him not trying hard enough to 'be good'. But in reality, he was not in complete control of what he ate and what he did: his parents were. And he was left to live with the consequences.

Heather helped her son to die and denied her first husband the chance to move back to their family home. But she did both of these things out of love, and care, and concern. The circumstances that unfolded before her weren't of her own doing or her own choice: her husband had a genetic illness that neither of them was aware of when they first got together, and she was left trying to make the best of a very hard situation.

We need to remember that life is rarely in our full control. All we can do is try our best and do what feels right at the time, and for the right reasons.

Don't waste time regretting the choices you've had to make in a certain moment, because it won't change a thing. Your time is precious. It should be spent, not wasted.

5. ACCEPT THAT EVERYONE MAKES MISTAKES (INCLUDING YOU) ... AND THEN SAY SORRY.

None of us are perfect. From time to time, we all make mistakes. Or make bad decisions, or say the wrong things. This is part of being human. If you have a functioning life where you talk, connect, or interact with other human beings, then the idea of never making a mistake is an impossible goal. Instead of wasting energy regretting your mistakes, own up to them, learn from the experience ... and say you're sorry.

Millicent was raised by a strict mum who ruled her world.

All those years later, at the age of 94, she still felt guilty and regretful about not telling the police what she had seen that summer's night. But she was a child then; she relied on her family for food and shelter. In those days you didn't defy your parents; you did as you were told. And knowing her mum was scared of having strangers in the house, and the effect that would have had on her family, could she really have gone against their wishes and gone to the police?

She made a mistake but that was her reality, and she tried her best to navigate it as best she could. She made a mistake, like we all do. And when we do, if we don't want to create a regret that lingers, we should try to recognise what we've done and why, and then apologise – honestly, and genuinely. Because the way we show people that we're really sorry isn't by berating ourselves; it's by admitting when we've done wrong, saying sorry and trying to never do it again.

Colin, my dad, regretted a lot of things. Not only what he told me years ago, about wishing he hadn't had children, but lots of other things that spanned many moments and decisions in his life. But he has now owned up to his past mistakes and apologised. The person he is today wouldn't make those same mistakes again. And him apologising and saying sorry has allowed him to be the best person he can be right now. Someone I love very much, and someone who I know loves me back.

Saying sorry is a very good thing, for both the apologiser and the recipient. Don't allow yourself to become imprisoned by your mistakes. It will shackle you to the person you've wronged and to a moment you'd probably both rather forget.

6. KEEP TRYING NEW THINGS.

New things, new places, new people … all of these are important. Because if you don't try new things once in a while, you may find your world getting smaller by default. You may find yourself shying away from taking chances, or taking the easy option in other areas of your life, too.

Annie had the opportunity to work on that cruise around the Caribbean.

Her friend was going and she wanted her to join her, but didn't. She didn't because not only had she fallen in love with a man she was worried about losing, she also wasn't used to doing new things. She was used to a steady, knowable life, just like her parents before her. Annie wished she'd gone. And all these years later she still feels that she'd let herself down, annoyed that she hadn't taken the same advice she gave to her kids: to go out and experience the world.

Doing things and getting out of our comfort zone is a habit. A muscle that needs flexing. The less we do, the less we'll want to do, or feel comfortable doing. And in this, the different areas of our lives can be connected: if you take a chance on a work project, then you'll be more likely to step out of your comfort zone and try new things, places and people. And 'new' doesn't have to mean big or expensive. It can mean trying a new dish when you get take-out, changing the route of your daily commute, choosing a different seat at your favourite café.

Something to remind ourselves that new or different isn't bad.

We are creatures of habit. Make sure your habits don't make you feel so safe and insulated that anything new or different starts to seem scary and impossible.

7. DON'T LET OTHER PEOPLE'S EXPECTATIONS GOVERN YOU.

Expectations can help us rise to our potential, or they can crush us whole. And when they come from other people, their effect can be ten-fold. Family, friends, partners ... they may all have an opinion on who you are and what you are (or aren't) capable of. In some ways it can feel like everyone knows us better than ourselves. Please remember: they rarely do.

Dee wanted to write, to be in love, to stay at home and raise her son. But she constantly put herself last. Her parents had left and her grandparents had no time for her. They, especially her grandmother showed Dee, that she should expect nothing: from herself, or anyone else. So that's what happened. Dee didn't give herself the time and space to do all the things in life she loved. Instead, she tried constantly to make other people happy, facilitating their dreams, and in the process neglecting her own.

Dee's grandmother was very direct in her many criticisms of her, but people can make their feelings and expectations known in a much more passive way.

Anthea's mum was constantly dieting and tanning her skin, burning it into a darker shade, trying to change into something else; a habit she then passed on to Anthea, which led her to develop a life-limiting melanoma. Anthea was raised in a house where keeping a man, and looking a certain way, were the most important things – even if that meant not safe-guarding her own daughter.

Anthea's mum taught her that she wasn't enough: in her looks, or in her being.

The constant nit-picking to be different, or the pressure to be 'the best', or to fit into a certain mould are expectations that can be very destructive. But as we get a little older and gain more autonomy, you have to try and remind yourself that you are who you decide you are. That you are enough. That you don't need to be a doctor or a lawyer to be happy. That you don't need to have a certain body or live a certain way to feel content.

Why can't we see all the lovely things we are? Why do we feel the need to change ourselves into something we're not, to weigh a certain amount, or to achieve a certain level of success until we feel worthy of living a good life?

You should never build the foundations of who you are on the expectations or views of others: your life is yours. Who you are, what you are worth and how you focus your time is up to you. The buck stops at your door. Never lose sight of that.

8. DON'T TRY AND REWRITE HISTORY.

Sometimes the choices and decisions we make, consciously or unconsciously, are an attempt to rectify the decisions we've made in the past, or the circumstances we've come from.

If the relationship that's just finished was controlling and critical, you might be drawn towards someone laid-back and positive as your next partner. If you come from a home without money or means, then creating wealth can become your loudest priority.

Just like Ada, Edmund and Alan.

Ada worked long and hard to build a successful business. She and her husband gave up a lot of their family life so they could work and create a healthy financial safety net. But in the end, when Ada looked back at how she'd spent her time and all her money was accounted for, she was left wondering if 'any of it was worth it'.

Edmund came from a childhood of need. Of scrabbling around for money and seeing people sleeping in doorways. Because of this, he was determined that he wouldn't have to live like that ever again. But his work and his need to bring in an income, and the worry he would slip and repeat history, meant he wasn't there for his wife when she needed him most. And because of that, she withdrew her love and he lost their marriage and home.

Alan wished he hadn't focused so much on driving himself on in business. He wished that he'd done something he might have enjoyed instead: teaching. But he wanted to prove his worth, to all the people who thought he couldn't work in tech; to all the people who doubted what he was truly capable of. He was trying to prove himself to people who didn't value what he did or who he was, and in the process got stuck on a corporate treadmill he felt unable to leave.

Sometimes we try and distance ourselves from the past, to make right what we thought was wrong. But when you do this, you can end up creating a whole new set of problems for the next generation to unravel.

Because the path we start on isn't freshly laid.

It's something that is shaped by our parents' lives, our parents' parents' circumstances, and also from the world and time we are born into. Our journey is ours, but not completely. And this, more than anything, when I think back to all the people I've talked to, is the overriding connector: that we all seem to be trying to undo, or make right, or rewrite the mistakes of our past. We seem to either look for the opposite of what didn't work in a bid to make good all the hurt, or keep choosing the same thing over and over again, hoping to change the outcome. And in the process, risk creating a whole new set of problems.

9. MAKE CONTENTMENT YOUR GOAL, NOT HAPPINESS.

This is something my grandmother always used to tell me and the older I get, the truer that statement reads: make contentment your goal, not happiness. It sounds like a cop-out at first – like we have to settle for one small step above being unhappy – but it's far from that. It's steady and real. And it can create a base for a lot of great moments and help cushion against the trickier ones.

Niall nearly died. He nearly lost his life, and his family nearly lost him, but the changes he wanted to make on the other side of his recovery weren't huge. He didn't want to do a 180 on his life because he was already pretty fulfilled, but now he could recognise the little things he'd been missing out on – like spending time with his kids and just enjoying their company. Doing that, spending time with them, had given him a contentment that his work and the rush-rush-rush of life hadn't been able to. Niall realised that the balance was off. That if you do less, then sometimes you have a chance to feel more.

Because the big moments in life may make us happy, but that happiness tends to be fleeting. We feel happy in the moment and then other emotions flood in – like stress, frustration, tiredness. To live a better, less regretful life, we have to try and get off the seesaw of happy/sad, or happy/bored, or happy/stressed and find a better balance, just like Niall did.

Happiness is great while it lasts. But when it comes to life, contentment can be king.

10. APPRECIATE THE EVERYDAY.

Most of us will spend more time in line at the supermarket or doing the school run than swimming with dolphins (sorry, dolphins!). But modern life seems to be slightly obsessed with these one-off extraordinary moments. That to 'find' ourselves, we have to go and stay in an ashram in India, or kneel at the feet of a shaman in Nepal; that travelling has to be off the beaten track and that work has to be making millions from creating a start-up from your kitchen table. Sometimes it can feel like if we're not doing something beautiful, or enriching, or impressive enough, then somehow we're not living at all. But listening to people nearing the end of their lives, it's the everyday things we seem to remember and cherish the most.

Tassia had always followed her heart. She didn't have any big regrets because she had 'never done a job I didn't enjoy and never had relationships I didn't like', so her regrets were firmly about the things she wouldn't be able to do now, rather than what she had already done; they were about the travels she wouldn't have, the studying that would never take place and the time she wouldn't get to share with her soon-to-be-husband, Nick.

The things that already had a place in her life.

It was the same for Katie. She might have some regrets over not appreciating what she had until they changed (her energy, her looks, her strength), but her decisions before that point – the man she fell in love with, the children they had together and the life they had built – were things she cherished. Her world was made of love, which is why she desperately didn't want it to end. And the things she was going to miss the most were the everyday moments: watching her kids grow up, growing old with her husband, seeing family and friends.

In the end, those are the things that seem to mean the most.

It's the day trips to the seaside, the first days at school, the chats over the back fence when we need a laugh or a helping hand. Because these are the stuff of life. And if we value one-off Insta-moments more than moments like this, more than the everyday, we risk not valuing the things that actually matter.

And the everyday can be wonderful, if we let it.

*

Regrets are the nagging reminder that we are running out of time. They are the things stamped in bold on the receipt of how we've spent our lives.

They are the travels not taken.

They are the ambitions left unfulfilled.

They are the things said, or unsaid.

Our regrets can lodge themselves in the gap between who we are and who we thought we would be; between what we have and what we thought we would have. They can live, and grow, and refuse to budge. Filling the present and future with the past.

So, is it possible to live a life without them? To get to the end of it all without looking back and regretting something we've said, or done; or something we didn't say or didn't do?

When I first started writing this book I thought the answer to that question was no. But after talking to so many people, and thinking back to what everyone has told me, I don't think the answer is an easy, clear-cut thing.

Because I think the answer is both yes *and* no.

It's yes, because it depends on what you consider to be a real regret.

And it's no, because if you are alive then you will make mistakes and missteps. That a life lived without regret isn't a life lived at all. That to get to the end with a clean slate and a completely clear conscience would mean you've made no mistakes and taken no chances. That you've spent your time skating around the outside of things, playing it safe.

Simon Ricketts didn't agree, He agreed with my first answer, of yes.

He was the only person who said they had no regrets at all, but that wasn't because he hadn't done anything 'wrong'. It wasn't because he hadn't made any missteps over the years. It was because he saw the whole idea of regrets, and of holding on to our decisions, differently.

He thought that if we try our best, and genuinely apologise when we fall short or have a lapse in judgement, then that is enough. He might have wished that his life would be many years longer, but he didn't regret what life he did have

– because his decisions and priorities were powered by love: love for his work, love for his partner. Love for his footballing community, his family and his friends.

And this seems to be the key to it all.

That how much and how long a regret is felt seems to be more connected by what powered you to make that choice in the first place rather than the actual choice itself. That if you make a decision based on love, based on trying to do your best for the people in your life that you love (rather than the people you're trying to impress or placate or prove wrong), then, whatever the outcome, any possible regret seems to take up less space.

Personally, I regretted a hell of a lot. At times, it felt that was all I did.

I wished I hadn't wasted so much time on a marriage that no longer worked.

I wished I hadn't given so much of myself trying to have another baby, or been so hard on myself for being 'unable' to keep the ones that I'd lost.

I wished I hadn't avoided parties and holidays, putting things off until I felt more confident, or had achieved more, or had lost those last 10lb (or 50lb!).

I wished I could have accepted myself for who I was, and had realised sooner that I was never going to be the person I imagined I would become when I was a child. And I really wished that I had realised that no one else seemed to judge me as harshly as I judged myself.

The truth is, some people are much better at dealing with the knocks of life than I am, but even I had got to the point when I had to say enough was enough. When I knew I couldn't keep focusing on what was wrong rather than what was right, or what I could change.

I wished that many things had been different, but they weren't. They were the way they were for a mixture of reasons – some of which I could have controlled, and some of which were passed down to me, or were a by-product of circumstance. But now they no longer hold me so tightly because I was honest about them and either reasoned them out, knowing I was simply doing the best I could with what I had been given, or I have set out to change them. Because I knew, in reality, our hopes and dreams don't always come true but that doesn't mean that a different version of them can't.

And there comes a point when you have to find a way to move on.

After lots of interviews, hundreds of miles travelled and hundreds of phone calls and emails, I have finally, exhaustively, come to that point.

I think I really needed to allow myself to be sad for what I had lost, but realised that I had to find a way to be happy and grateful for what I already had: for my child, my good health and all that me and my ex had shared during our 22 years together.

The drink had been drunk and the nibbles were nibbled and the pity party was over.

And I am very aware that there are millions of people out there who have been through so much more than me; unimaginable things that no one should have to experience. But from speaking to the dying, from people who had also been through so much, I realised that if we want to try and find some contentment, then we need to try to find a way to live with these moments. To live *beside* them rather than *in* them. Because if we don't, then we risk not living at all. We risk merely existing. And we owe it to ourselves and the people we have lost and the things we've had to endure to do more than just exist.

That if we are alive, then we have to find a way to properly live.

Because we are still here, and at some point, we will run out of summers – we all will.

Death really is the only guarantee and yet we run from the idea of it, we deny its existence because it's a hard thing to comprehend – that we can be here, living and breathing, and then gone forever. But if we accept that there is an end, then we are much less likely to be in a position to regret things as we would use our time more wisely. We wouldn't keep putting things off until some perfect, fantastical moment – because, deep down, we know there isn't one. As Annie said, 'You are never, ever sorted because life throws stuff at you that unsorts you.' So, you, we, all of us have to find a way to just get on with it.

What happened to that trip you've always been meaning to take?

What about that concert you put off, or that friend you keep meaning to meet up with?

Sometimes it feels like we will live forever, because at this moment in time we find ourselves fit and able, our bodies and our minds functioning and doing what we ask of them. But deep down we know that this is a lie. A sweet, negotiated lie to fool ourselves into a false sense of foreverness. Life is not an egg timer: we don't get to run out of days and turn it over and start again. It's an unknown, finite thing.

The sand is already falling and we have to – we need to – make the most of what's left.

I've met too many people who were living a 'normal' life one year and were gone the next to know we shouldn't take tomorrow for granted. None of us should. Because none of us ever truly knows how many more days and nights we have left, how many more summers.

We put things off, thinking one day there will be a perfect moment, a moment when things will feel easier. But there isn't, and there probably never will be.

If we avoid swimming or dating because we feel 'too fat' …

If we don't go to that party because we don't have any nice clothes to wear …

If we don't attend that school reunion because we feel like our life won't measure up …

If we don't change jobs or set up a business because we're scared of failure …

If we don't tell people how we truly feel about them in case we are rejected …

Then we are wasting time and missing out on potential experiences that we may never get to enjoy again. All we have is right now. We need to go swimming, and go to that party; to start dancing, and learn how to cook; to ask the questions we always wanted to ask; to travel to the places we've always wanted to go to; to have more sex; to experiment and to take a chance on love. We all need to stop thinking and planning, and actually start doing,

Whether it's having children, not having children; giving up on a love, or staying in a relationship for too long; working too much, or pursuing the 'wrong' dreams; not putting down roots, or letting those roots confine us. Whether it's not having enough confidence or trying to make right the world you were born into, I think we all do things we regret. Things we would wish we had or hadn't done given our time again. It may be the fact you never got to travel, or you weren't as successful as you thought you'd be. Or maybe your life didn't turn out quite how you imagined it would.

Maybe you aren't as brilliant, tall, slim, smart, rich or popular as you'd hoped you'd be. Or perhaps you just felt like you were too busy, too caught up in the day-to-day to make the most of things when you had them and now wish you'd been more present and available.

That you were always looking forward or behind, but never at right now.

In the end, maybe we all have something we look back on and regret. Maybe some of us manage to move on and be pragmatic about the things we can't change and others hold those things close and don't let go. Maybe they can't, and maybe that's fine, too.

Maybe all we can do is live well but not try to live too perfectly. To take chances as they arrive and not put things off. To make the most of all that we can, but also know that we can't live each day as if it were our last because that would be exhausting.

To take time to be truly honest with ourselves and ask: Am I happy with my life?

To be honest about the things we're content with and the things we'd like to change, as well as the things we are ready to appreciate that little bit more.

And most of all, to remember, that in the end, when we've lived our lives and our number is up, it's the little things that stay with us: the chances we've taken, the people we've loved and the moments we've shared. That it's really about love.

It was always about love.

Love is the thing that drives our lives, even when we don't realise it.

Love for our family, our friends, ourselves. For our work and our community. For our hobbies and passions. For our faith, in whatever form that may take.

Love seems to be the difference between a lingering regret, or a regret being let go of.

Love is what makes the difference.

*

The chances are by the time you've read this, some of the people you have met in this book may have already died. I will be forever grateful that they have allowed me to share their thoughts and words with you, especially as they knew their time was limited.

It's hard getting to know someone – in person or on the page – knowing that there is nothing you can do to change their situation. That their one wild and precious life will be over. That their year to live will be done.

So, put yourself in their shoes for a moment and wonder: what would I do, what would any of us do, if we were given more time to live? Because whatever else you think is lacking in your life, whatever changes you wish to make right now, you still have that – you still have time.

You still have choices to make and roads to travel.

Now, you get to decide where those roads will take you.

Goodbye to All That

I hope, by the time you've reached this final chapter, that the stories you've read will have helped you in some way. That if you're facing your own regrets, or find yourself at a crossroads, or even if you're just questioning why you are here or what you're doing with your life, that you may have gained some clarity.

You may, like me, have come to realise that some of your old regrets, wishes and ambitions are no longer relevant. That you now feel able to gently set them aside and allow yourself to appreciate, and enjoy, what you already have. Or maybe you've been able to see what you want with more focus and are ready to start building a practical plan of action to help get you there.

Whatever situation you find yourself in, I hope you may now feel able to say goodbye to all that. To all the things that have come before. That in reading these reminders of how finite our time is, you feel emboldened to build something new, or simply appreciate and be happy with what you already have.

And if you ever find yourself in doubt, if you ever find yourself double-guessing whether you're on the right path or not, stop and ask: If I had a year to live, what would I do with it?

If you're truly honest with yourself, the answer will guide you home.

'What a wonderful life I've had!
I only wish I'd realised it sooner.'

— *Colette* —

Acknowledgements

Writing may be a solitary affair but publishing, and getting a book out into the world, is not. Lots of people have helped in lots of different ways.

Thanks to my friends and family for all their support: in particular to my brilliant mum, Elinor Brown, Harriet Pike, Andrew Wright, Lisa Bruce-Tamakloe, Marc Beattie, Douglas Coombes, Richard Lock, AP, Mike and Jo Lock, and my dad.

To Dr Jonathan Rohrer for his advice on FTD; Dignity in Dying; Brain Tumour Research UK; and the Huntington's Disease Association. And to Acast for hosting my podcast where a handful of these stories first appeared, and Adam Macaulay and the drama team at Radio New Zealand for commissioning a play which led me to find Millicent and Edmund.

Thanks also to Alexandra Allden for creating such a beautiful cover; Jane Donovan for making sure my errors (of which there were many) were so thoughtfully corrected; and Ailsa McKillop who transcribed all of my interviews with such care.

To Sophie Herdman for connecting me with my agent; to my agent, Richard Pike, for his amazing faith and guidance; and to my editor, Oli Holden-Rea, for all his great notes and invaluable encouragement.

To CC for all their patience and love.

And most of all, thank you to all the people that have allowed me to step into their world. Words cannot fully express how much I appreciate them sharing their time, their thoughts, and their wisdom.

Notes

1 Brain Tumour Research www.braintumourresearch.org
2 Wikipedia, *British Shipbuilders*, viewed September 2021 https://en.wikipedia.org/wiki/British_Shipbuilders
3 Brain Tumour Research www.braintumourresearch.org
4 National Brain Tumour Society www.braintumor.org
5 World Health Organisation *Coronavirus Dashboard*, viewed October 2021 https://covid19.who.int
6 Alzheimer's Research UK, *Getting a Genetic Test*, viewed October 21 https://www.alzheimersresearchuk.org/blog/getting-a-genetic-test-for-familial-alzheimers-disease-at-25